How to Attain Your Desires

By Letting Your Subconscious Mind Work For You

Joe Vitale Presents...

Attaining Your Desires
by GENEVIEVE BEHREND

For information about permission to reproduce
selections from the book, write to Permissions,
Morgan James Publishing, Post Office Box 6504,
Newport News, Virginia 23606-0504

ISBN: 0-9758570-8-8

MORGAN · JAMES
PUBLISHING FOR THE REST OF US...
www.morganjamespublishing.com

Printed in the United States of America

How to Attain Your Desires
By Letting Your Subconscious Mind Work For You

2004

JOE VITALE
GENEVIEVE BEHREND

JOE VITALE

CONTENTS

INTRODUCTION vii

Attaining Your Desires 1

DEDICATION 3

FOREWORD 5

LESSON I: INTERPRETING THE WORD...................... 21

LESSON II: HOW TO GET WHAT YOU WANT 29

LESSON III: HOW TO OVERCOME ADVERSE CONDITIONS 43

LESSON IV: STRENGTHENING YOUR WILL 59

LESSON V: MAKING YOUR SUBJECTIVE MIND WORK FOR YOU 69

LESSON VI: HOURLY HELPS 89

LESSON VII: PUTTING YOUR LESSONS INTO PRACTICE 97

Hypnotic Marketing Library Collection from Joe Vitale 99

About the Authors 119

INTRODUCTION

When I moved from Houston to my current Hill Country estate, I only packed three books with me -- out of my collection of 5,000 -- for the trip. One of them was Genevieve Behrend's incredible little book, *Attaining Your Desires*, first published in 1929 and now long out of print and forgotten.

I found a rare copy of this amazing book many years ago. It profoundly influenced my life. It taught me how to focus on the *essence* of something I wanted---rather than on the *appearance* of something---in order to magnetize myself to receive what I truly desired.

As a result of using Genevieve's methods---simple as they may seem---I've manifested new cars, new homes, a new relationship, improved health, book sales, passive income, and a whole lot more.

My friend David Garfinkel, master copywriter, said this about this little book:

"I would say this is the clearest, most comprehensive, most practical and indeed most do-able explanation of how the Creative Process works in real life that I've ever read."

The person who typed the book for me from the original (so I could turn it into an e-Book and later publish it) wrote this:

"I've never seen a book like this before! It's inspiring me to pick what I want and showing me how to get it! Thank you for letting me type this book! THANK YOU!"

And my webmaster read over the book and wrote me saying:

"This is an amazing little book!"

What's the story on this almost miraculous old book?

Genevieve Behrend wrote her book as a complete seven-lesson course in the early 1920s. The writing is in dialogue form, between a "Sage" and a "Pupil." The Sage is the famous author and teacher, Judge Thomas Troward; the Pupil is you. It is very easy reading, very tightly written, and very enlightening.

Within these lessons is pure compressed dynamite. Here are a few sub-headings to give you a sense of the staggering power of this rare material:

"The Secret of Controlling Your Life Forces"

"Don't Look for Coincidences In Your Life"

"How to Drive Anxiety Out of Your Mind"

"How You Can Control Circumstances"

"How Your Mind Is Related to The Universal Mind"

"How to Develop Health and Harmony"

The list of incredible topics, answers, and mind expanding concepts goes on and on. The book even includes special sections on handling anger, disease, disappointment, and much more.

You can now learn from this amazing author, too. I've taken Genevieve Behrend's magical book, hired a typist to input the entire book, and am now releasing it the public as the book you are now holding – for the first time in almost a hundred years.

You may have read books on manifestation before---maybe even my own *Spiritual Marketing* book---but I GUARANTEE you've never read a book like THIS one before.

When Bob Proctor (who wrote the foreword to *Spiritual Marketing*) and I were talking one day about the books that influenced us, he asked me if I ever heard of the little known book by Genevieve Behrend. Bob had never seen the book, but had heard rumors of it. I told him I not only heard of it, I OWNED one of the few original copies of it in existence it. I later gave Bob a photocopy of the book as a gift.

But you now own a copy of the actual book.

Start imagining what life will be like for you once you know how to attain your desires.

You're about to learn the secret to making all your wishes come true.

What will be your first wish?

Magically,

Dr. Joe Vitale
www.MrFire.com

PS -- Most people know of Genevieve Behrend's first book, *Your Invisible Power*, which is still in print, but almost no one knows of her second, much more rare and powerful book. With it you can manifest just about anything you can imagine. And you are now holding it in your hands!

PPS -- What were the other two books I took with me when I left Houston? The first was the now legendary *Robert Collier Letter Book*. The second was Christian Godefroy's book *How to Write Letters That Sell*. And the third, of course, was the one you are now reading. Consider: If Genevieve Behrend's book is so good that it was one of only three books I pulled from my collection of 5,000, shouldn't you at least take a look at it and maybe tell friends about it, too?

JOE VITALE

Attaining Your Desires

By Letting Your Subconscious Mind Work for You

By

GENEVIEVE BEHREND

L. N. FOWLER & COMPANY
7, IMPERIAL ARCADE, LUDGATE CIRCUS
LONDON, E.C., ENGLAND

Originally Published by

THE ELIZABETH TOWNE COMPANY

Incorporated

HOLYOKE, MASS., U.S.A.

DEDICATION

"There shall never one lost good!
What was, shall live as before."

— *Browning.*

"I know that, whatsoever God doeth, it shall be
forever: nothing can be put to it, nor anything

taken from it. That which hath been is now;

and that which is to be hath already been; and
God requireth that which is past."

Ecclesiastes 3: 14, 15.

These pages, the outpouring of a full heart, I lay
reverently upon the memory altar of a man who
was sage and saint, teacher and guide, and my
dearly beloved friend, Judge Thomas T. Troward.

FOREWORD

"All we have willed or hoped or dreamed of good, shall exist, Not its semblance, but itself."

— Browning.

"The thing that hath been, it is that which shall be; and that which is done is that which shall be done."

—Ecclesiastes 1:9

THE sages of the centuries, each one tincturing his thought with his own soul essence, have united in telling us that, "As a man thinketh in his heart, so is he." It has been established by the experience of the ages that always the law is the same. But HOW shall one think in his heart, so that only goodness may blossom and ripen into rich deed and rare result? What is the apparently mysterious secret by which life's dull metal is transmuted into precious mintage?

It is my purpose to tell you in this little book. I desire to crystallize the heart-coinings of my revered master, Judge Thomas T. Troward, as reflected through the mirror of my mind and soul. I have adopted as my means of expression, the dialogue style, familiar to all students of that greatest of all speculative philosophers, Plato. I am convinced, through years of study of this almost superhuman mind, that this literary form is the one most nearly calculated to convey the most subtle shades of meaning, the richest depth of soul-sounding. I know that my readers will agree with me that if they will put themselves in my place, as students, and let me answer them as my master answered me, it will clarify their interest and intensify their joy in these lessons.

What I wish particularly to convey to you within these pages is the method of scientific right thinking, and to awaken in you the desire to try to use this method in order to form the habit of thinking ONLY the thoughts you wish to see crystallized in a worthy achievement or result. In addition, I want to direct your thoughts toward a better understanding of that Spirit of God, or Good, which points the way to the roseate dawn of a new civilization. The rapidity with which the ideas of man are changing causes humanity to realize that this new civilization is already manifesting itself through a clearer understanding of the relation between man and his Maker.

The epochal keynote of the present generation is that mind is the kingdom in which man reigns supreme. As the poet says, "A brute I might have been, but I would not sink i' the scale." In endeavoring to make conscious use of thought-power, causing it to produce desired material results, mankind is beginning to understand the indispensability of absolute control.

My chief idea in sending forth this message is to make it easier for you to live in hourly consciousness that you have been given dominion over every adverse circumstance and condition which may arise. The conscious use of the creative power of thought to protect and guide you, as well as to provide for you, is only attainable through understanding the "natural relations between mental action and material conditions."

Your reading of these lessons should be with a steadfast determination to think rationally and effectively on every word, in order that the full meaning of each thought may be thoroughly grasped and comprehended. Thought-power is the kingdom of God in us, always creating results in our physical forms corresponding to our normal sustained thought. As Troward has said, "Thought is the only action of the mind. By your habitual thoughts you create corresponding external physical conditions, because you thereby create the nucleus which attracts to itself its own correspondence, in due order, until the finished work is manifested on the material plane."

This is the principle upon which we shall proceed to work out a simple and rational basis of thought and action whereby we may bring into outer expression any desired goal. Let us work together to this end.

— G.B.

TROWARD-PHILOSOPHER AND SAGE

ONE of the really great minds and souls of modern times-and indeed of any time-was Thomas Troward, late Divisional Judge of the Punjab, India. Of his writings, the late William James of Harvard said, "Far and away the ablest statement of that psychology that I have ever met, beautiful in its sustained clearness of thought and style, a really classic statement."   The *Boston Transcript* editorially stated, "The author reveals himself as easily the profoundest thinker we have ever met on this subject." The late Archdeacon Wilberforce, when writing to Troward, signed himself, "Your grateful pupil."

Responding to the many requests from Troward's friends and admirers for a more intimate glimpse of this great man, I am pleased to present to you a few phases of his daily life as I saw them while studying with him. These may be all the more interesting because of the fact that I enjoyed the unique privilege of being the only pupil to whom he ever gave personal instruction.

THE EARLY LIFE OF A GENIUS

Thomas Troward was born in Ceylon, India, in the year 1847, of English parents and Huguenot ancestors. When quite a young boy he was sent to England to be educated at Burmshtead Grammar School, but was most unhappy there, as he could not fully adapt himself to the humdrum life of the English schoolboy. Later on, when he continued his education in the beautiful Isle of Jersey, its charm entered into his blood, and he was thoroughly contended there.

Perhaps the old Huguenot strain in him found a congenial element in the semi-French environment of the college. At the early age of eighteen the natural bent of his mind began to assert itself, and he won the Helford College gold medal for literature.

When his studies were completed, Troward went up to London for the Indian Civil Service examination, a very stiff one, which he passed with high credit. He returned to India at the age of twenty-two in the capacity of Assistance Commissioner. An incident which occurred during the course of his examination foreshadowed the trend of the life that was to replace the regulation judicial career when the twenty-five years of service had expired.

"YOUR HEAD IS NO COMMON ONE, YOUNG MAN"

One of the subjects, left for the end of the examination, was metaphysics. Troward was quite unprepared for this, having had no time for research and no knowledge of what books to read on the subject, so he meditated upon it in the early hours of the morning, and filled in the paper with his own speculations. The examiner, on reading it, was amazed, and asked, "What text-book did you use for this paper?"

"I had no test-book, sir." Troward answered. "I wrote it out of my head."

"Well, then, young man," was the examiner's comment, "your head is no common one, and if I am not mistaken, we shall hear from you again."

During Troward's career in India his official work kept him very busy. His recreation was often spent with canvas, paints and brushes. He was an artist of no mean ability, especially in marine subjects, and had won several prizes at art exhibits in England. He loved to study the tomes of sacred Indian lore, or the scriptures of the Hebrews and of other ancient peoples. While studying these profound subjects, there was unfolded to him, as in a vision, a system of philosophy which carried with it not only peace of mind, but also physical results in health and happiness.

When relieved of his burdensome official duties in the Indian Court, he returned to England, where a manuscript of some hundred folios slowly came into existence. At that time he had no knowledge of Mental Science, Christian Science, New Thought, or any of the "isms" of modern thought. His views were the result of solitary meditation and a deep study of the scriptures. The first edition of the now famous "Edinburgh Lectures" was published in 1904. It was received with the almost unanimous opinion that its value could not be overestimated, as was true of his subsequent volumes. "Bible Mystery and Bible Meaning" proved especially attractive to churchmen. His books, by sheer worth, have found their way almost all over the world. In the United States alone, more than 50,000 copies have been sold. Perhaps no one was more astonished at their warm reception that their simple-hearted, fun-loving author.

AN INTIMATE DESCRIPTION

In physique Judge Troward was not the usual English type, but was more like a Frenchman, of medium stature, and not over five feet six or seven inches. He was dark complexioned, with small, bright eyes, a large nose, and a broad forehead. When I knew him, he had a drooping mustache sprinkled with grey. He had the bearing of a student and a thinker, as is indicated in his writings.

His manner was simple and natural, and he exemplified a spirit of moderation in all things. I never saw him impatient or heard him express an unkind word, and with his family he was always gentle and considerate. He seemed to depend entirely upon Mrs. Troward for the household management. Only in the intimacy of his home did he entirely reveal his charming geniality and radiating friendship. His after-dinner manner was one of quiet levity and a twinkling humor. He would enter into the conversations or parlor games of the family with the spirit of a boy. He did not care for public amusements.

One evening, after an excellent dinner of soup, joint of lamb, vegetables, salad, dessert, and wine, he rolled a cigarette, and, to my great surprise, offered it to me with the query, "Do you smoke?" Receiving a negative reply, he began to smoke it himself. Noticing my poorly concealed expression of surprise, he remarked, "Why should you be shocked at anything which you can thank God for? I can thank God for one cigarette after, possibly a second, but never a third." After he had finished his smoke, his youngest daughter, Budeia, played the violin for us. I observed that he became completely absorbed in the beautiful harmony. He told me afterwards that, although he was intensely fond of listening to music, he was in no sense a musician.

Although Troward did not indulge in outdoor sports, he loved nature, and would sit for hours by the sea with his sketch-book, or tramp the lonely moors in solitary meditation. He said there were times when he obtained his best inspiration while walking in the open. He often invited me to go with him, although frequently he seemed to be unconscious of my presence, being entirely absorbed in his own thoughts.

TRUTH FROM THE TRANCE

At times he would lapse into a trancelike swoon (his Maltese cat on the table by his side), the swoon sometimes lasting for hours. At such times the members of his family would take particular care not to disturb him. When he emerged from these lapses of the senses, he would write down the truths which had been revealed to him. Once he wrote on his memorandum pad, " 'I AM' is the word of power. If you think your thought is powerful, your thought is powerful."

It may be interesting to recall that such authorities as Barnett and the new American Encyclopedia, in their biography of Socrates, mention similar trancelike experiences of his. While serving in the Greek army, Socrates suddenly found his feet seemingly rooted to the earth, where he remained in a trance for twenty-four hours. He awakened with a spiritual knowledge that transformed his life, and, later, the lives of many others. The similarity of the life of this Athenian philosopher to that of Troward is that both relied chiefly upon intuition and common sense for their theory and system of living.

A difference between Troward's teaching and that of Christian Science is that he does not deny the existence of a material world. On the contrary, he teaches that *all physical existence is a concrete corresponding manifestation of the thought which gave it birth.* One is a complement of the other.

I once asked him how one could impart to others the deep truths which he taught. "By being them," he answered. "My motto is, 'Being, and not possessing, is the great joy of living.'"

FOLLOWING A TRUSTED GUIDE

Judge Troward, although modest and retiring in his habits of speech and slow to express a personal opinion, was always willing to discuss any current subject, but extremely reticent and diffident about his own writings. Never, to my knowledge, did he mention them unless approached on the subject. As a teacher, he was positive, direct, and always impersonal.

When our lesson was given indoors, he always sat in a large morris chair, and, seeming not to be aware of my presence, he would think aloud. To follow his thought was like following a trusted guide through the most difficult places, the darkest and least explored regions of thought. As I followed, the personality of the man became obscure, and I was only conscious of the clear, commanding voice, and the light of the inward torch which he bore. It was beyond doubt quite natural that he who made so clear the true meaning of individuality should in his teaching betray little of the personal or emotional element.

After I had been carefully guided to the most comforting conclusions, in the same quiet, unassuming manner as in the beginning of our mental journey, my guide would gently remind me that he had given me a few suggestions which I might follow if I felt inclined, but which were offered only in the friendly spirit of a fellow-traveler. He always tried to impress upon me that every effort to accomplish mental control (which, in turn, meant control of circumstances) should be undertaken with absolute confidence of success.

The length of a lesson depended upon my ability to absorb what he was telling me. If he were convinced in fifteen or thirty minutes that I understood quite naturally the reason why, for example, "If a thing is true, there is a way in which it is true," that lesson was concluded. If it took me an hour or more to get into the spirit of his thought, the lesson was prolonged. At the end of a lesson he would quietly remark, "Never forget that 'seeking' has 'finding' as its correlative: 'knocking,' 'opening.'" With this reassuring statement, he would light his lantern and step into the denseness of the night to walk three miles to his home.

A HOME-LOVING PHILOSOPHER

Being a home-loving man, Troward delighted in his flower garden, and in the intimacy of his home, which he had provided with every comfort. He particularly enjoyed the seclusion of his studio and his study, which were arranged to meet his personal needs and moods. His studio was in the most remote part of the house, and here he would spend hours of relaxation with canvas and paints. His study, however, was on the ground floor, and to it he would retire for meditation and research, usually in the early hours of the morning. He rarely worked at night.

He had spent the greater part of the day he died sketching out of doors. When he did not join his family at the dinner hour, Mrs. Troward went in search of him. She found him in his studio, fully dressed, lying on the sofa in a state of physical collapse. About an hour later he passed away. The doctor said that death was caused by hemorrhage of the brain. I am sure that Troward would have said, "I am simply passing from the limited to the unlimited." He died on May 16th, 1916, in his sixty-ninth year, on the same day that Archdeacon Wilberforce was laid at rest in Westminster Abbey. It was no ordinary link that bound these two men, as you will note in the reproduction of the letter which follows, Troward's last letter to me.

Thomas Troward regarded death very much as he would regard traveling from one country to another. He remarked to me several times, that he was interested in the life beyond and was ready to go. His only concern seemed to be the sorrow that it would cause his wife and family. When the time came, his going was exactly what he would have wished it to be.

I hope that these few intimate touches will give to Troward's friends and admirers the information they desire concerning him. I will add a more personal touch for you by presenting herein one of his first letters to me with facsimile of his handwriting.

31 Stanwick Rd.,
West Kensington,
8th Nov. 1912

DEAR MRS. SWINK,

I think I had better write you a few lines with regard to your proposed studies with me as I should be sorry for you to be under any misapprehension and so to suffer any disappointment.

I have studied the subject now for several years, and have a general acquaintance with the leading features of most of the systems which unfortunately occupy attention in many circles at the present time, such as Theosophy, the Tarot, the Kabala, and the like, and I have no hesitation in saying that to the best of my judgment all sorts and descriptions of so-called occult study are in direct opposition to the real Life-giving Truth; and therefore you must not expect any teaching on such lines as these. We hear a great deal in these days about "Initiation"; but, believe me, the more you try to become a so-called "Initiate" the further you will put yourself from *Living Life*. I speak after many years of careful study and consideration when I say that the Bible and its Revelation of Christ is the one thing really worth studying, and that is a subject large enough in all conscience, embracing as it does our outward life of everyday concerns, and also the inner springs of our life and all that we can in general terms conceive of the life in the unseen after putting off the body at death.

You have expressed a very great degree of confidence in my teaching, and if your confidence is such that you wish, as you say, to put yourself entirely under my guidance I can only accept it as a very serious responsibility, and should have to ask you to exhibit that confidence by refusing to look into such so-called "mysteries" as I would forbid you to look into. I am speaking from experience; but the result will be that much of my teaching will appear to be very simple, perhaps to some extent dogmatic, and you will say you had heard much of it before. Faith in God, Prayer and Worship, Approach to the Father through Christ—all this is *in a certain sense* familiar to you; and all I can hope to do is perhaps to throw a little more light on these subjects, so that they become to you, not merely traditional words, but *present living facts*. I have been thus explicit, as I do not want you to have any disappointment; and also I should say that our so-called "studies" will be only friendly conversations at such times as we can fit them in, either you coming to our house or I to yours as may be most convenient at the time. Also I will lend you some books which will be helpful, but they are very few and in no sense "occult."

Now if all this falls in with your own ideas, we shall, I am sure, be very glad to see you at Ruan Minor, and you will find that the residents there, though few, are very friendly and the neighbourhood is pretty. But on the other hand if you feel that you want some other sort of learning, do not mind saying so; only you will never find any substitute for Christ.

I trust you will not mind my writing to you like this, but I don't want you to come all the way down to Cornwall and then be disappointed.

With kind regards

Yours sincerely,

(Signed) T. TROWARD

ATTAINING YOUR DESIRES

AS TOLD BY

THE SAGE TO HIS PUPIL

THE SAGE: T. Troward's philosophy as taught to his only personal pupil, Genevieve Behrend.

THE PUPIL: Humanity at large.

LESSON I: INTERPRETING THE WORD

FEELING that an explanation of some of the words employed in an unusual way in these lessons may be helpful to the student, I herein offer a list of such words, together with my interpretation and references from Troward.

Absolute

"That which is free from limit, restriction, or qualification." (Webster.) "An idea from which the elements of time and space are entirely absent." (Troward.)

Example: Thinking in the absolute would be simply dwelling upon the intrinsic qualities of love without reference to whom you love or the various forms through which love expresses itself.

Mind is absolute because of its self-reaction.

Being

Life, that unformed power of life which controls circumstances and conditions. Read Troward's "Bible Meaning and Bible Mystery," pages 77-79.

Belief

A certain quality in the creative power of thought, which manifests on the external plane in exact correspondence to the quality of belief entertained. If you believe that your body is subject to disease, then the creative power of the thought of disease results in a diseased body. Read Troward's "Edinburgh Lectures of Mental Science," page 14.

Body

The instrument through which thoughts and feelings are expressed. The envelope of the soul.

Brain

The instrument through and in which the action of the Universal Parent Mind expresses itself in specific form as individual thoughts. Brain is not the mind, but the mind's instrument.

Christ

A state of consciousness which is altogether good, and a quality of feeling which manifests in physical form. The most perfect spiritual concept.

Circumstances

The outward effect which corresponds to the inward tendency of thought.

Conception

William James says ". . .denotes neither the mental state nor what the mental state signifies, but the relation between the two."

Concentration

"Bringing the mind into a condition of equilibrium which enables us to consciously direct the flow of spirit to a definite, recognized purpose and then carefully to guard our thoughts from inducing a flow in the opposite direction."—"Edinburgh Lectures on Mental Science," page 88. (Troward.)

Conditions

The result of mental tendencies. Harmonious thought produces harmonious physical and material conditions, which still further react to sweeten thought.

Consciousness

Activity of mind which enables it to distinguish itself from the physical form in which it manifests.

Create

To bring into existence. Thought is creative, because it always brings into physical or objective existence forms which correspond to itself.

Death

Absence of life. Loss of consciousness, with no capacity to regain it. Example: If a thought has been absolutely eliminated from the consciousness and cannot be recalled, it is dead to you.

Faith

"The divine promises and individual faith are correlations." Combine them, and there is no limit to what you can do through the creative power in this quality of thought.

"Essential thought. Therefore every call to have faith in God is a call to have faith in the power of your own thought about God." (Troward)

A confident expectant attitude of mind. Such a mental attitude renders your mind receptive to the creative action of the spirit of life. Have faith in the force of your own thought. You have many times experienced what it will do. Jesus' statement, "Have faith in God and nothing shall be impossible unto you," is not a mere figure of speech; it is a scientific fact, simply stated. Your individual thought is the specialized working of the creative power of life. (All Life.)

Intelligence

The Universal Infinite Mind. The highest intelligence is that mind which understands itself as the instrument through which the Intelligence which brought it into existence operates.

Love

Universal Life and Universal Law are one.

The law of your being (your life) is that you are made in the image of God (the Creative Power which brought you into existence) because you are God's very self specialized.

The law of your life is that your mind is "the individualization of Universal Mind at the state of self-evolution in which your mind attains the capacity for reasoning from the seen to the unseen and thus penetrating behind the veil of outward appearance. So because of the reproduction of the divine creative faculty in yourself, your mental states or modes of thought are bound to externalize themselves in your body and in your circumstances." (Troward.)

Spirit

It is impossible to analyze the nature of Spirit (or Life), but we can realize that whatever else Spirit may be, it is a self-creating power which acts and reacts upon itself, reproducing itself in inconceivable forms from the cosmos to man. (Just as your mind acts and reacts upon itself when you are memorizing.)

Origin of all visible things.

As it is independent of time and space, it must be pure thought, the embodiment of stored consciousness.

A self-acting and self-reacting non-physical creative power or force. Its action can only be *thought*, because thought is the only conceivable non-physical action.

Thought

The specialized action of the original, creative Spirit or Mind.

Truth

That which lives in you is truth to you.

Visualizing

Inward or mental vision. (Visioning). Life's creating power taking particular form. The act of producing in your mind the picture of any contemplated idea.

Word

Your individual thought is the specialized word or action of the originating mind-power itself.

"That which starts the etheric vibration of life moving in a special direction," corresponding to the word, which originates special movement.

"The seed which gives rise to the thing." Plant your word-seed in the Subjective Mind of the universe, and you are sure to receive a corresponding thing, just as truly as poppy seed produces poppies.

Faith gives substance to things unseen.   (The unseen word or thought.)

LESSON II: HOW TO GET WHAT YOU WANT

"Ye shall know the truth and the truth shall make you free."—*St. John 8:32.*

SAGE: If a thing is true, there is a *definite* way in which it is true. And the truest thing in Life is that it contains inherent within itself absolute joy and liberty of mind, body, and affairs.

PUPIL: Do you mean that my understanding of Life's laws can give me the realization of perfect liberty in my individual life?

SAGE: Yes, providing you do not make the common error of judging everything from a material standpoint only. Recent research in physical science has established the fact that there is enough power in a lump of clay to destroy a city. All the average mind is able to see is the inert clay, whereas, in reality, it is the physical instrument which contains the invisible power.

PUPIL: Then when I understand the law of vibration, I can get anything I want; achieve anything I desire?

SAGE: Life fills all space, and through the understanding and use of Life's laws, you can give direction to a particular quality of creative force, which, if held in place by the will, is absolutely certain to reproduce in a corresponding physical form. What every human being wants is more liberty and more joy in life. From whatever angle you study the subject of Life, you will find that degrees of livingness and liberty are invariably manifested by varying degrees of intelligence. What you would term inanimate life represents the lower forms of intelligence; in plant life you recognize a higher degree of intelligence. To illustrate this, look at a flower. Is it not beautiful? Does it not prove to you the indisputable presence of a Great Intelligence which is expressing itself as beauty, form, and color, and, above all, joy?

PUPIL: Yes.

SAGE: Still you will not find it difficult to recognize in the animal kingdom a quality of Life and Intelligence which is greatly in advance of that manifested in the flower. Then the intelligence which expresses itself in the mind of man as the power of initiative and selection is the highest expression of Intelligent Life. Thus you see that the inanimate, the plant, the animal, and the human all represent the same Universal Life, the only difference being in the varying degrees of intelligence. For example: You are expressing a very high degree of intelligence in desiring to understand the laws of Life. When you have discovered some part of these laws, you will ascend the scale of intelligence as you make practical application of your discoveries. Another example: Two men leave college with the same degrees and situated very similarly relative to social and financial position. Both study the laws of Mind; both are obliged to struggle. One, by making a great mental effort, keeps mentally above the discouraging conditions, and finally comes into a smooth road, while the other one becomes disheartened and ill, barely eking out a miserable existence. You can readily see where the higher form of intelligence was manifested in these two cases.

Intelligence was there, but it could only grow by being used constructively.

HOW DEGREES OF INTELLIGENCE
PROVE MAN'S PLACE IN THE
UNIVERSE

SAGE: The greater your intelligence, the more easily you can call into action the highest order of creative energy. The more highly you develop your intelligence (and I do not mean by this intellectuality or book learning—I mean self-education) the more you will find your old limited ideas of what you are not, cannot be, do, or have, imperceptibly slipping away. By using your intelligence and resting upon it to guide you Godward, you will come to recognize that you are as much a part of the very *highest* Intelligence as a drop of water is a part of the ocean. This steady recognition on your part, carried into your everyday affairs, will give you control over adverse circumstances, which you realize are, after all, only effects of lower degrees of intelligence, and will deliver you from falling a victim of a material universe. You are *not* a victim; you are a part of the Universe.

PUPIL: Just what do you mean by "effects of lower degrees of intelligence"?

SAGE: I mean, by a lower degree of intelligence, one that is unable to recognize itself as being one of the highest forms of life. The highest degree of intelligence is that form of life which is able to recognize itself as related to all existing Intelligence. For example: You can easily recall the last difficult situation you came through. It was the expression of the highest form of Intelligence which enabled you to think your way out of that.

THE INTELLIGENCE WHICH DISTINGUISHES US
FROM THE APE

SAGE: You recognized your difficulty, but you also recognized your intelligence as being able to draw to itself, from out the whole Universe, ways and means of meeting that perplexing problem. The Law is ever the same. When you are convinced that every physical circumstance or thing has its origin in corresponding activities of the mind (thought), you are able to conquer adversity in any form, because you know you can always control your thoughts. You must always be determined do to your *own* thinking.

PUPIL: It is not difficult for me to understand that the flower is the result of some invisible power, which must be Intelligence, but for me to realize that this same life and intelligent power in *my* life is not easy. I had not been taught to think in this way. However, you have made me realize that if I wish to learn, I must put into practice the directions you have given me. So when I needed to have five hundred dollars at a certain time and could not see any possible *means* of getting it, I tried to follow your instructions by mentally seeing myself as doing the thing I wished to do. I visualized myself paying my obligation, and in some way, which is still a mystery, I was able to feel quite calm about it. I made my mental picture and actually forgot to worry about the ways and means, and the money came. I did not quite understand then, and I do not know now, jut how it happened. All that I am able to realize is that, by my obedience to your teaching, the day was saved for me, and I shall not forget it.

Now I would like to know if we inherit our tendencies of mind?

SAGE: Most of us inherit our thoughts, just as we inherit the color of our eyes. If you intend to understand "the relation existing between mental action and material conditions" sufficiently well to control your circumstances, you must think for yourself, and in your own way, irrespective of that your ancestors thought, even though some of them might have brought desired results.

PUPIL: That seems as impossible as reaching the horizon. However, if you tell me that I can arrive at the place where circumstances and conditions will be under my control, through a steady and determined effort to find out the truth along these lines, I *shall* do my own thinking from this moment. My present condition, however, seems beyond the control of any human being, much less myself, and there have been times when I did control certain conditions, but at other times the same conditions were beyond my control. Why was that?

THE SECRET OF CONTROLLING YOUR
LIFE FORCES

SAGE: The reason you succeeded, without understanding the power which you possessed, was that you used it unconsciously, according to the law of its own nature, and reached harmonious results (as in the incident that you have just related). Your ability, at all times, to use the unfailing power which is yours depends upon your recognition of its presence. The reason for your times of failure is that the distressing condition so wholly absorbs your attention that you are unable to think of anything else. At such times you entirely lose sight of the fact that your individual mind is the instrument through and in which the very highest form of intelligence and unfailing power is endeavoring to express itself. Also, that it always takes the form of your habitual thought. Therefore, when you believe that a situation is beyond your control, so it is.

PUPIL: Which means that my control of circumstances is entirely measured by my capacity to know that the life and intelligence in me is the same Life and Intelligence which brought me into existence? The same Life in the trees and all nature, and I tune in with all Life? Will this steady recognition give me direct contact with *all the power and intelligence which exists?* Would simply dwelling on this thought solve any situation which might arise?

SAGE: No. "Faith without works is dead." God without expression is a nonentity. Thought without action is powerless. But your *recognition* that you are inseparably connected with the *joy, life, intelligence,* and *power* of the Great Whole, *unwaveringly maintained* and *carried into practical application,* will solve any problem, because your thought calls into specific action ideas of the very highest degree of intelligence and power, which naturally controls the lesser degrees. "The lesser modes of life are in bondage to the law of their own being because they do not know the law." Therefore, when you know the Laws of Life, this knowledge gives you ideas which enable you to control all adverse circumstances and conditions.

PUPIL: This is all so new to me, I do not quite grasp your meaning. Will you please give me an illustration?

HOW TO LIGHT THE PATHWAY OF
YOUR LIFE

SAGE: Well, suppose you were in a room where every comfort had been provided for you, but the room was in total darkness, and you were unable to locate the things you desired, although you were conscious of their presence. You were told that the room was electrically lighted, and instinctively you began to grope your way along the wall, where you were accustomed to look for a light switch. For hours you passed your hands up and down the walls as far as you would reach until you were quite fatigued. You were about to give up the search and make the best of a bad situation, but, overlapping this thought, there came the resolve that you would not abandon your effort until you had located it. You were determined to enjoy the good things awaiting you, so you renewed your search with the feeling of assurance that ultimately you would find a way to turn on the light.

After more fruitless endeavor, you paused to rest, and to wonder where that switch could possibly be. "It must be here, and I shall find it," you said to yourself, and again you passed your hands over the walls, although you felt certain that you had gone over every inch you could reach. This time your thoughts and movements were not quite so tense, although equally determined. As your hands moved slowly up and down, your mind caught the idea that the switch might not be on the wall at all. You paused a moment, and the suggestion that it might be on the floor registered in your consciousness. But reason stepped in and argued, "Impossible. Who ever head of a light switch being placed on the floor!"

"But," the suggestion persisted, "why not try? You have gone over what first seemed the most reasonable places to find it. Try the floor."

So then you began to reach out uncertainly with your feet for some projection on the floor which might be a light switch.

FINDING THE LIGHT

Almost instantly your feet came into contact with an unfamiliar object. You put your hand on what seemed to be a push button, but no light appeared. Nevertheless, you now felt quite *sure* that you had located the switch. You paused, and involuntarily asked yourself, "How does this thing work? It won't push and it won't pull." Back came the answer within yourself like a spoken word. "Sidewise." You moved it sidewise, and the room was flooded with light. Your joy at thus finding a responsive intelligence within yourself could not be expressed in words. It was a rapture of the heart which many have felt at times.

PUPIL: Oh, I am so glad that the switch was found through clinging to the right mental attitude! Does such persistent effort always meet with such a satisfactory reward?

SAGE: Yes, persistent, confident endeavor *always* brings satisfaction. In order to give you a complete picture from which you may logically reason in the future, let us consider the same situation from an opposite angle.

Imagine yourself in the same room under the same conditions. After several attempts at feeling around in the dark, you begin to feel tired, more or less discouraged, and you reason with yourself thus, "Oh, what is the use? There *may* be a light switch in this room, and the room *may* contain everything I require, and again it *may* not." But something indefinable in yourself convinces you that not only is the light there, but so, also, are the things you enjoy and desire. You answer right back to yourself, "Well, if everything is here which I need and would enjoy, what a pity that I *cannot* find the switch! What a strange and unreasonable way some people have of doing things! I wonder why the light was not already turned on for me."

PUPIL: You make it seem that one almost involuntarily and invariably blames circumstances or people for his failures!"

"THE FAULT, DEAR BRUTUS, LIES NOT
IN THE STARS, BUT IN OURSELVES,
THAT WE ARE UNDERLINGS"

SAGE: You must admit that it is rare to find anyone who realizes that the cause of his failure or continued misfortune lies within himself. The reason for this is an almost universal lack of understanding on the part of the individual that a certain quality of thought brings to the consciousness a recognition of an intelligent power capable of attracting to him, and directing him to, the fulfillment of his purpose and the attainment of his desire. On the other hand, the inversion of this same power effects a negative result.

PUPIL: You mean that a certain quality of thought enables one to do and be what he wishes, while the misuse of the same power seems to thwart one's purpose?

SAGE: Yes. The idea is to use your power of thought and feeling positively, in order to attain positive results. Use it negatively, and you get negative results, because the unchangeable law is, "Intelligence always manifests in responsiveness." The whole action of the evolutionary process of Life, from its first inanimate beginning up to its manifestation in human form, is one continual intelligent response.

If you would induce yourself to recognize the presence of a Universal Intelligence which permeates all nature, you must also recognize a corresponding responsiveness hidden deep down in all things—in the trees, the weeds, and flowers, in the animals, and, in fact, in everything—which is ever ready to spring into action when appealed to. It will respond to your call as a child would obey when bidden to come and play.

In your first experience in the dark room, your all-absorbing thought was not so much about the darkness as about the light, and how it *could* be turned on. The positive "I will" quality of your thought brought up from the depth of your inmost soul a steady flow of intelligent power, which finally penetrated through to your intellect and guided your hand to the switch.

PUPIL: But the second time when I also thought I *must* find the switch, there was no enlightened response. It seems to me that this is one's everyday experience. The first case seems like a miraculous coincidence.

DON'T LOOK FOR COINCIDENCES IN

LIFE

EVERY EFFECT HAS ITS CAUSE

SAGE: Oh, no. *All* is Life, and all is law and order. There are no coincidences in reality, no "happen so's." You will realize this if you will recall some of your own experiences similar to the ones used in the illustrations. You often feel that you must have "light," and, after several attempts to avail yourself of it, your thought and feeling settle into the "I cannot do it" groove; "it may be possible for those who know how, but I don't," etc. The best method of learning the truth about this is to live your past experiences over again. Analyze what your thoughts and feelings were when you succeeded, and when you failed. Then draw your own deductions. No written or spoken words equal this kind of instruction.

Remember that all space is filled with a responsive Intelligence and Power ever ready to take any form which your sustaining thought-demand creates. This power can work only in terms of the thought instrument through which it operates. Humanity generally admits Jesus' ability, Jesus' power to use the spirit of intelligent life to produce material conditions—as in turning water into wine, but they doubt their ability to use the same Power in themselves, in spite of Jesus' assurance, "All things are possible unto *you*." Now this statement is either true or false. If true it is because your mind is the instrument in and through which this intelligent Principle of Life takes initiative action, and this action, in turn, is always in accordance with the laws of life, which are subjective in their nature.

LIFE'S GREATEST PURPOSE IS TO
EXPRESS JOY, BEAUTY, AND POWER

PUPIL: Am I right in concluding that this lesson in life, which is an ever-present, limitless, intelligent power, is ready at all times to be guided in any direction that my sustained thought may give it? If I permit to be anxious, discouraged, dissatisfied, I bring into action repelling, destructive forces? Life's purpose is to give expression to Its joy, beauty, and power, through Its particular instrument, my thought. Is this right?

SAGE: You have grasped the letter of the lesson in a remarkable way. Now it remains only for you to experience the happiness of what you have learned. Do this putting by your knowledge to practical application, never losing sight of the fact that no matter *what justification you may think you have at the time, any feeling of discouragement, dissatisfaction, or anxiety causes the fulfillment of your right desire to recede further and further away from you.* Whereas, by *persistent and determined endeavor* to trust your own desires and ambitions as the specific expression of the universal loving, guiding, and protecting Principle, you will find that your supply for their fulfillment will unfold to you greater and greater liberty in every direction.

PUPIL: When one does not wish to entertain negative thoughts, how can the sense of discouragement and anxiety be shut out? I am sure that it is not because one enjoys feeling worried that it seems so difficult to eliminate it. Do you mean that it is as possible to snap out of a thought one doesn't want as it is to step from one room to another? I should like to know how that is accomplished, as I have many unwelcome thoughts which I am wholly unable to dismiss at the time. After a period they leave, but it seems to me they use their own sweet will about it. I have honestly tried to rid myself of thoughts, which seemed to cling all the tighter when I tried to throw them off. It would be wonderful to cast off a thought as one would a garment! How can it be done?

SAGE: By keeping a *positive attitude of mind* regarding your innermost desire as *an accomplished fact*, whether it be for a state of mind or for a thing. You cannot think positive and negative thoughts at the same time.

PUPIL: Oh, is that true? It seems to me I have often been speaking to someone on a certain subject while my thoughts were on an entirely different one.

YOU CAN ACTUALLY THINK OF ONLY ONE THING AT A TIME

SAGE: You were *thinking* one thing and *saying* another. You had only *one* thought. You automatically said one thing while thinking another. In short, your words were not the expression of the thought in your mind. Suppose you give yourself a test; try to think of yourself as a success and a failure at the same time. You will find it impossible to think positively and negatively simultaneously. In our next lesson we will take this up more extensively and prove why it is true. Also why you, as an individual, can control circumstances, whether they be mental, physical, or financial, through the understanding of your personal relationship to the Intelligence which governs the universe.

PUPIL: I know that what you say is true, but just what method should I employ to accomplish this? There are times when I become cross and impatient with myself because I give way to anxiety and fear (the very things which I know *now* will cause my defeat). And yet I will do it, just as I will eat something I like even though I know it will disagree with me. Could you give me a formula to use at such times?

HOW TO DRIVE ANXIETY OUT OF YOUR MIND

SAGE: When the triad of enemies-fear, anxiety, and discouragement-assails you, poisoning your mind and body, weakening your power to attract what you want, begin instantly to take deep breaths, and repeat as fast as you can, aloud or silently, the following affirmation, which is an antidote to the poison and a powerful assurance and attraction of Good:

The Life in me is inseverably connected with all the life that exists, and it is entirely devoted to my personal advancement.

If you are alert and can make this affirmative thought overlap the negative, anxious suggestion, you will very soon free yourself. If the tendency to dwell on these erroneous beliefs keeps recurring, go where you can be alone, repeat your affirmation, and endeavor to lift your mind up to your words, much as you would lift your breath from the bottom to the top of your lungs. Never be impatient with yourself because you do not quite succeed in your every endeavor. It is your *intention* that counts, not necessarily the *absolute fulfillment* of the letter. The ALL-KNOWING POWER THAT IS understands and rewards accordingly. Be *diligent* and *patient*, and you *will surely succeed*.

LESSON III: HOW TO OVERCOME ADVERSE CONDITIONS

"There is nothing either good or bad, but thinking makes it so."—*Shakespeare*.

SAGE: If you wish to overcome adverse conditions or to maintain a favorable one, it is necessary to have some knowledge of the fundamental or originating Spirit, and your relation to It. The true order of these fundamental principles of life which you are endeavoring to understand does not require you to deny the reality of the existing physical world, or to call it an illusion. On the contrary, *by admitting the existence of the physical, you thereby see the completion of a great invisible, creative process.* This enables you to assign physical manifestations to their proper places in the creative series, which your former way of thinking did not enable you to do. You now realize that, while the origin of life is not in itself physical or material, it must throw out physical and material vehicles through which to function as its means of expression, in varying degrees of intelligence, such as the vegetable or the animal kingdom, and the human, as illustrated in our last lesson. All are forms of life, because of that inner Principle of being which sustains them. The Life Principle with which you are primarily concerned is the *life of thought and feeling in yourself. You are a vehicle or distributing medium of the creative Spirit of Life.* If you understand this, you will have some idea of what the originating Spirit of Life is in Itself, and your relation to It as an individual.

PUPIL: Since thought and feeling are the origin of all things, would it not be necessary to get into the spirit of their origin in order to control circumstances? Is it true that my thoughts and feelings are the same as those of the limitless Power and Intelligence of the universe?

HOW YOU CAN CONTROL CIRCUMSTANCES
AND ERRONEOUS CONDITIONS

SAGE: In essence they are the same. You are able to control the circumstances and conditions relative to your individual world, *of which you are the center*, by making your thoughts and feelings correspondent in quality (at least in a degree) to what you believe are those of the originating, intelligent forces of life.

PUPIL: Is it true that the life in me contains everything that I, as an individual, could ever require? Are my thoughts and feelings the centralizing power of my particular world? If so, then Browning explains the situation when he says, "We carry within us the wonders we seek without us." If I know and practice this great fact, the wonder of Life's understanding power will come forth in me by its own divine right, and assume command over all my problems in exactly the same degree that I recognize it. Is that correct?

SAGE: Yes, Browning has voiced the truth in that sentence. The divine Principle in you is complete, and is the only Life there is. But this should not lead you into the error of believing that you are not to exert yourself. Remember that the life-germ in you is an Intelligence which can call into specific action all of life's forces from out the entire universe, but it can only work through *your* intelligence in correspondence to what you *confidently believe* it *can* and *will do*. Therefore, be practical in your reasoning, and diligent in your deeds.

Suppose I give you an example: You have a glass of dirty water. In order to have the clear water, you would continue to pour the clean water into the glass of dirty water until every drop of the dirty water had flowed out of it, wouldn't you? The same rule applies to adverse conditions. Pour into them a steady stream of confidence in the power of God in you to change them, and they *will* change, correspondingly.

PUPIL: I understand. You mean that I should use my common sense, coupled with a steady faith in God and earnest, concentrated mental effort?

COMMON SENSE AND YOUR MENTAL FACULTIES

SAGE: That is it. Use your common sense and all your mental faculties as far as they will take you. However, you should never try to force a situation. Always allow for the Law of Growth. Remember that conditions will grow into the correlative shape of your firmly held mental attitude "under the guidance of the All-Creating Wisdom." If you will follow this method of reasoning, you will soon form the habit of examining your own attitude of mind for the key to your progress and enjoyment of life. Endeavor to keep before your mind's eye the thought that every physical or material condition in your life corresponds to your habitual thought tendency, and your thought tendency will eventually become the reproduction of the way you regard your personal life, as related to all life.

PUPIL: Shall I be able to overcome one limitation after another, as I develop the knowledge and feeling of regarding the Life Principle in me as the source of all physical experience? As I advance along these lines, shall I grow into the liberty of enjoying life in my own way?

SAGE: In studying the law of your own being, the important thing to realize is that you, as an individual, are a specializing center, through which the power or essence of Life takes forms which correspond exactly to your most habitual conceptions. Try to realize more and more thoroughly, both in theory and in practice, that the relation between your individual mind and the Universal Parent Mind is one of reciprocal action. Grasp the principle of reciprocity, and you will comprehend why you fall short sometimes of enjoying life, and how you can attain to full enjoyment; just as the law of gravitation shows why iron sinks in water, and can also be made to float.

PUPIL: It is rather difficult for me to understand what you mean by the reciprocal action between my individual mind and the Universal Parent Mind. Suppose I am facing a big financial problem, and I endeavor to bring my mind into a state of confident expectancy through meditation upon the ever-present supply in all forms of life, and by repeating an affirmation which seems logical. Would that do it? Where does the reaction come in? And how? If my happiness in life depends upon this understanding, and upon living in a state of conscious reciprocity with the Parent Mind, it seems just now that it is a long way off, because I do not grasp your meaning. Should I feel a reaction within myself when striving for a certain state of consciousness?

HOW YOUR MIND IS RELATED TO THE UNIVERSAL MIND

SAGE: We said in our last lesson that your mind was an outcome of the great Universal Parent Mind which brought you into existence for the direct purpose of expressing Itself through you. The reciprocal action between your mind and the Parent Mind might be compared with a tree and its branches. Your mind is the *specific* expression of the Universal Mind from which it draws its power to think, just as a branch of a tree is a specific part of a tree, not apart *from* it, but a part *of* it. Thus, between the Universal Mind or Life and its own specialized expression (which is your mind), there is a perpetual interaction, as with the tree and its parts; its branches and its leaves are continually drawing sustenance from the parent trunk. Your thought action is the specialized, identical action of the Universal Mind.

Example: Imagine yourself feeling a bit downcast, when suddenly you are handed a telegram with the news that the one person in the world whom you love the most is on his way to see you, and the messenger of some wonderful news! Can you not imagine what a definite reaction you would have from news like that?! Well, you can stimulate the same quality of thought, that same feeling of joy and surety between your individual mind and its source, through mentally picturing yourself as doing the things that you enjoy. See yourself happy, and lift your mind up to it by constantly repeating a happy affirmation, and you will readily realize the reaction in kind.

PUPIL: I see. The way that adverse conditions are to be overcome is through my recognition of the reciprocal action going on continually between my mind and the One great Universal Mind, which brings about the same kind of a reaction that I would have from an agreeable experience on the physical plane. I used to think that conditions were overcome by ignoring them, and setting aside the inherent law that caused them. I begin to realize now (theoretically at least) that the laws of life cannot be ignored nor destroyed, but, on the contrary, must be made to work for us to produce a harmonious existence.

SAGE: Adverse circumstances are overcome by reversing the originating cause, which is your own thought. Anxiety and fear always attract conditions of their own kind. Reverse this tendency and entertain only those thoughts which register harmony and confident assurance, and the adverse circumstances will recede, and in their place will appear the conditions which correspond to your changed mentality.

PUPIL: Am I to regard my mind as a branch of the Universal Mind from which I draw all my substance?

SAGE: Yes. You now have a fairly good general idea of the two ultimates: the Universal and the individual, and their relation to each other. I think we should now consider the process of specialization, that is, how to make nature's laws produce a particular effect which "could not be produced under the simple generic conditions *spontaneously* provided by nature."

HOW TO REMEDY NATURE'S SHORTCOMINGS

PUPIL: How can one create conditions not provided by nature?

SAGE: Do not overlook the word "spontaneous." By consciously and intelligently arranging your thoughts in the new order, by looking within yourself for the solutions of your problems, instead of without, you will certainly find that ideas will come to you, which, if followed, will produce new conditions other than those provided by nature.

PUPIL: How can I do this? Is this brought about by causing my thoughts to correspond to those which I think the Universal Mind must have?

SAGE: Let me give you an illustration of what I mean. Take the case of a miller who has been grinding his grain by hand. His instinctive feeling is that there should be a more efficient way of grinding grain, and he meditates a good deal on what this way might be. One day, while walking in the country, his attention is attracted, for the first time, to the power in a stream of water as it rushes past him. He pauses, and reflects on how this power could be utilized for his particular purpose.

"Why not harness it and make it grind my grain?" he asks himself. This unexpected inspiration thrills him through and through, not only because of its possibilities, but because of his feeling of assurance that it can be accomplished. Immediately, the desired result begins to picture itself in his mind. By the side of the stream he sees his gristmill working under new conditions, with a great wheel attached to it revolved by the force of the running water, and thus grinding his grain. The force of the water *spontaneously* provided by nature has not been changed; it has been specialized to meet an individual requirement.

HOW NATURE WORKING THROUGH MIND CAN GRIND THE GRAIN

PUPIL: Naturally the power of the water could not of itself have ground the grain, but through the interaction of the individualized Universal Intelligence in the miller's mind, he made this power "spontaneously provided by nature" do his bidding, just as Burbank specialized nature's laws by making cactus grow without thorns, and blackberries without seeds.

SAGE: Yes, you have grasped my meaning. Your comprehension of the interaction between the water-power, or nature, and the individualized Intelligence in the mind of man is scientifically correct. You see now that it is an entire reversal of your old conception. Formerly, you took forms and conditions as symbols, and inferred that they were the causes of mental states and material conditions; now you are learning that the true order of the creative process is exactly the reverse, that thought and feeling are the originating causes which form corresponding external conditions. This is the foundation principle upon which you can specialize the generic law of the whole creative process, and cause it to bring all of its Intelligence and Power to bear, in meeting your particular necessity.

SHOWING THE SILVER LINING OF THE CLOUD

PUPIL: You are right. I have been inverting the order of cause and effect. It always seemed to me that conditions both created and controlled my thoughts, that is, I involuntarily accepted the thoughts which the conditions suggested.

For example: Suppose I want to be at a certain place at a certain time. My appointment is important and I shall be late. What a terrible thing it will be! There seems nothing to be done. That is the way I used to think.

Now, in the new order of thinking, I shall endeavor to mentally see myself as keeping my appointment, etc. I shall get into the spirit of the thought that nothing can impede my progress or thwart my purpose, and I am sure that a way will open enabling me to materialize this thought on the physical plane. I am sure that in some unforeseen way my engagement will be kept, satisfactorily to myself and to the other person. In fact, I have experienced similar episodes.

SAGE: Yes, almost everyone has had such experiences as you have related, but very few profit by them. The law is, "As a man thinks so it becomes." If you wish to withdraw from an undesirable situation, you must adopt the scientific method of affirmative thinking, and follow it up as a permanent factor in life.

You will find that the universal causative Power (call it what you will) always manifests as supreme Intelligence in the adaptation of means to ends. For instance, there is something which you wish to do—build a house, sell something, or do a kind act for someone. It is this supreme Intelligence manifested through you that guides your activities. Without it, you would be unable to outline your intention, much less accomplish your purpose. Your intelligence is the instrument through which the One Great Intelligence of the universe is constantly taking specific form. This being true, every idea which registers in your mind was first formed in this One Infinite Mind. A continual recognition of this fact will enable you to find your way out of any sense of limitation which may arise in your individual experience.

I once heard of a man who had an intense desire to do big things. He asked his teacher to think with him along the lines just discussed—that the Intelligence of the universe was taking specific form in his individual intelligence. His teacher agreed providing the student's desire was great enough to force him to arise every morning and take a two-mile walk, meanwhile meditating upon this interaction between the Universal Intelligence and its special form, his mind. The student also was instructed to form the practice of making mental pictures for the precise purpose of developing his intuition and imagination. One suggestion was that he should mentally see himself walking along a beautiful, clear, flowing river, hearing the rippling water, and seeing the reflection of the trees on its clear surface, and then to transfer his mental picture to one depicting his own desire.

After following this practice for six months, an idea of almost overwhelming magnitude came to his mind. This did not seem unnatural, however, as it was so completely in accord with his recent habit of picturing his all-absorbing desire. He joyously continued his walks, his meditation, and visualization, and finally the Universal Intelligence manifested in its specific form (his mind) by giving specific directions to bring the big idea into successful operation.

PUPIL: Could his mind have captured this big idea without the help of a teacher?

ALWAYS LEARN TO DO YOUR OWN THINKING

SAGE: Certainly. The idea did not come through the teacher's mind; he simply started the student on the right track. No one can think for another. It was the result of his determined effort to recognize his own individual intelligence as the instrument in which the Greater Intelligence was constantly taking form. All that the teacher did (all that anyone could do) was to help him to hold his thought along the path he desired to go. The help of the teacher strengthened his conviction and faith in the power in himself.

PUPIL: Is this originating power of life a forming power as well as a creating and directing one, and did the teacher's thinking along the same lines steady the student's thoughts? Without the support of a more advanced mind, could anyone succeed in a great undertaking?

SAGE: Certainly. *If you are sufficiently convinced of the absolute truth of your method, you do not need any sustaining force outside of your own conviction.* You miss the point of your relationship to the great whole if you do not realize that it is not only an originating, but also a forming power. Do you not recognize its forming power throughout nature? You would not think of trying to make a lily a rose. If you know that the same Power that created the flowers also made your mind for the specific purpose of operating in it, you would soon learn to trust its formative nature in its operation through your intelligence.

PUPIL: I understand. It is the power of Life in man which originates, creates, directs, and forms. In reality, there seems to be nothing whatever for man to do in this great scheme of things except to enjoy life, if he can only learn how!

GOD AND COMPANY, LTD.

SAGE: The Law of Life is God and Company. You are the Company, and you cannot in any sense be an idle partner, if you wish to profit by the partnership. Your part is a big one, and there is plenty for you to do in providing a concrete center around which the universal divine energies can operate.

PUPIL: Does this mean that to realize my oneness with the joy of life I shall not find it as simple as it seems?

SAGE: No doubt there will be times when you will find it difficult to transfer your thought from externals to the interior realm of the originating principle, and to joyfully hold it there until external conditions correspond with the ideas you have in mind, but there should never be any strain. You are attracted to the Universal Mind as your source of supply, along the lines of least resistance. That is to say, along these lines which are the most natural to your individual and particular bent of mind. In this way you infuse into the Universal Mind your desires and ambitions, thus intensifying your power of attraction (relative to the desire uppermost in your mind) from the infinite forces.

For instance, let us suppose that you feel very much alone, not altogether lonely, but alone (there is a difference, you know), and yearn for congenial companionship. At a certain night and morning, go where you will not be interrupted, and mentally picture yourself walking with a companionable friend (no person whom you know, but an ideal one); then see yourself riding with this same friend, and the two of you doing many happy things together. Keep your picture in mind until all sense of aloneness has disappeared, and you *feel* an unmistakable sense of companionship. Let that feeling register in your consciousness, and try to recall it at will. If you will practice in this way, you will very soon realize that this is the reciprocal action between your mind and the Universal Mind. Once this recognition is well established, *your* ideals will begin to express themselves in form.

PUPIL: Then one's efforts should be wholly directed to the attainment of a higher degree of intelligence, rather than to the acquiring of material things.

"GOD WILL PROVIDE THE FOOD, BUT
HE WILL NOT COOK THE DINNER"

SAGE: Such a purpose is the very highest, and aspirations along this line would surely externalize corresponding things. Under no circumstances should you allow yourself to form the habit of idle dreaming. The material side of life should not be despised, for it is the outside of a corresponding inside, and has its place. The thing to guard against is the acquiring of material possessions as your ultimate aim. However, when certain external facts appear in the circle of your life, you should work with them diligently and with common sense. Remember that things are symbols, and that the thing symbolized is more important than the symbol itself. "God will provide the food, but He will not cook the dinner."

PUPIL: My part then is to cook the dinner, so to speak; to use the intelligence with which I have been endowed, by making it a power to attract, from out the universe, ideas that will provide for me in any direction that I may choose to go, according to law?

SAGE: Yes, if you choose to go with life's continual, harmonious movement, you will find that the more you use the law of harmony through progressive thinking, the more intimately acquainted you will become with the law of reciprocity. This law corresponds to the same principles which govern physical science; that is, "nature obeys you precisely in the same degree as you obey nature." This knowledge always leads to liberty.

PUPIL: How does nature obey me?

SAGE: Nature's first and greatest law is harmony. You see the results of harmonious law in the beautiful world around you. If you obey nature's suggestion, and follow the law you will be the recipient of all the benefits contained in this law of harmony that nature has to offer, such as health, strength, contentment, etc., for all of her laws bring freedom and harmony. You will find nature responding along the same lines, to the extent that your thoughts and acts are in accordance with her perfect laws.

PUPIL: Is the power of thought always creative, and does it always create conditions corresponding to itself? Can one know this law sufficiently well to cause it to respond immediately?

FIFTEEN MINUTES NIGHT AND DAY ARE NOT ENOUGH

SAGE: Thought as thought is always creative, either good or bad. The length of time required for the corresponding physical conditions to appear in the circle of your individual environment depends entirely upon your ability to recognize that your desired course is a normal, already existing, mental fact. It is not enough to get into the spirit of your reasoning for fifteen minutes night and morning, with the inward confidence that you are directing a certain, unfailing power toward a desired physical manifestation, and then spend the remainder of your waking moments in doubt and fear. The whole question is, how does your particular sustained thought affect you? If it stimulates your feeling of faith, the response is immediate.

PUPIL: Could you give me something to memorize which will help me to eliminate doubt and fear?

SAGE: Yes. The thought I use most frequently myself is this:

"My mind is a center of divine operation. The divine operation is always for expansion and fuller expression, and this means the production of something beyond what has gone before, something entirely new, not included in past experience, though proceeding out of it by an orderly sequence of growth. Therefore, since the divine cannot change the inherent nature, it must operate in the same manner in me: consequently, in my own special world, of which I am the center, it will move forward to produce new conditions always in advance of any that have gone before." (Dore Lectures)

You should memorize this passage and meditate upon it, endeavoring to make your mind a "center of divine operation," by entertaining only such thoughts as you feel are reflections of God's thoughts. Whenever you sense that your way to freedom is obstructed, make a stronger endeavor to live with the spirit of your affirmation, and you will soon find your mind receiving ideas, which, if followed, will guide you into the path of absolute liberty.

THE DEVILS OF DOUBT AND FEAR

PUPIL: Doubt and fear are the devil, are they not? Is not fear the most destructive of all wrong elements? It seems to me that it is ever present in one form or another. Can this monster be entirely eliminated from one's mind?

SAGE: Surely. Although fear is the most destructive of all the mental enemies, and, as you say, seems to be ever present, yet when you realize that your *fear is just as certain to materialize as is your faith*, you will grow more and more guarded as to the quality of thought which you harbor. Practice makes perfect.

PUPIL: Try as I will to inhibit fear, I am unable to succeed at present. At times I utterly fail, and I am overwhelmed with it.

HOW TO DRIVE OUT FEAR

SAGE: The moment you begin to feel fearful, get into the open if possible, walk briskly for a mile or two, taking deep breaths, and holding your chin in and chest up. Think of yourself as a monarch of all you survey and assume a corresponding commanding attitude. Repeat with every breath this affirmation: "I am breathing in the Life, the Love, and the Power of the universe RIGHT NOW!" Hold the breath a second, with the affirmation in the center of your mind; then expel the breath with the same thought and send it out to mingle with the ether of the universe. "I and my Father of Love are ONE."

If you cannot get out into the open, assume, wherever you are, the same attitude. Take deep breaths, repeat the affirmation, and you *feel* certain that you are protected and supplied with all the love and power which Life has to give, fear will disappear, and you can resume whatever you were doing.

LESSON IV: STRENGTHENING YOUR WILL

"All we have willed or hoped or dreamed of good, shall exist; Not its semblance, but itself; no beauty, nor good, nor power Whose voice has gone forth, but each survives for the melodist, When eternity affirms the conception of an hour."

—Browning.

SAGE: The importance of the will is so frequently misunderstood that I think we will consider its true nature and purpose for a while this morning. Almost everyone is conscious that willing is not imagining. What the function of the will is, for the most part, baffles and escapes our reasoning.

PUPIL: I understand that most schools of mental science teach that one should not try to use or even understand the will, because to make conscious use of will-power leads one astray.

SAGE: It is most important that you should have sufficient knowledge of your will not to misuse it, or to be led astray through lack of understanding its place and power.

PUPIL: Is it a compelling, creative power?

SAGE: Correctly speaking, the will is neither one. It is in no sense creative. There are times, however, when a strong will can compel certain external combinations.

PUPIL: If will-power can produce certain external results, why not use it to that end?

SAGE: Because I was not intended to be used in this way. Conditions brought into existence by mere force of will lack vitality; consequently, the situations brought about by simple will-power disappear as soon as the will relaxes.

PUPIL: Do the things which are forced into being through the power of a strong will disappear simply because they lack vitality, or because the compelling power relinquishes its hold?

SAGE: Both, because of the lack of any real life in them, and because the energy of the will which supports them is withdrawn.

PUPIL: I have read a great deal about the function of the will. What does it mean?

THE ACTION OR FUNCTION OF THE WILL

SAGE: It depends upon what you have read about the different kinds of will. The will is the power-control in your mind, which holds your thought in a given direction until a result has been accomplished.

For example: Suppose you wish to go to a certain place; without the will to go there, you could not even start, nor could you retain the thought of the place long enough to arrive. You would start in the right direction, and then, because there was no sustaining power in the thought, you might turn and go in another direction.

PUPIL: So it is the will which holds thought to a given purpose until it is consummated; or keeps an idea in its place in one's mind until it is objectified in form. It might be termed a thought-stabilizer.

SAGE: Just so. It is the will which holds your mental faculties in position relative to the creative power which does the desired work. Thought is always creative, as I have explained in my book "The Edinburgh Lectures on Mental Science," page 84: "If, using the word in its widest sense, we may say that the imagination is the creative function, we may call the will the centralizing principle, *its* function being to keep the imagination centered in the right direction." The will has much the same place in our mental machinery that the tool-holder has in a power-lathe. To my mind this is the will.

PUPIL: It is a wonderfully clear statement. It means that success or failure is contingent upon but one thing: *mental control*, and the will is this controlling factor.

SAGE: The business of the will is always the same, that of keeping your mental faculties where they will do the work you intend them to do.

PUPIL: Suppose I were conducting a business, but my thoughts were more on an anticipated vacation than on my work. Naturally my business would suffer. How could my will help me?

PRACTICE "WILL EXERCISES"

SAGE: The case you relate illustrates a weak will. You know that your thoughts should be kept on your business, but your will is too weak to do it. You should practice will exercises to strengthen your mental energies. These will help you to focus your attention on business or any desired activity.

PUPIL: If one concentrated his entire attention on business during business hours, would he be able to relax it later and enjoy his home and play?

SAGE: With a properly trained will, you can pick up a thought at choice, hold it until it has finished its work, let it go again, and then pick up another thought, repeating the process again and again if you choose. In short, you can work when you work and play when you play.

PUPIL: No doubt it can be done, but it seems to me now that it would be a terrible strain.

SAGE: On the contrary, the well-trained, developed will maintains any position you desire without any strain on the nervous system, and its use is never followed by a sense of fatigue.

PUPIL: I have always found it a great strain to hold on to any thought which did not abide in consciousness naturally.

SAGE: This is an indication of a weak will, which should be strengthened through exercise, the beginning of which should be "a calm, peaceful determination to retain a certain mental attitude in spite of all temptations to the contrary, knowing that by doing so, the desired result will surely appear."

PUPIL: Is the will intelligent?

"A DEVELOPED WILL IS THE HANDMAID OF INTELLIGENCE"

SAGE: The developed will is the handmaid of Intelligence.

PUPIL: What do you mean by that?

SAGE: In training your will, you will become conscious of the presence of a tremendous power which acts on the plans of the very beginning, or first cause, of every so-called physical thing. This power is the primary Living Intelligence of the universe. Tell yourself what you desire in a clear, concise way, confidently knowing that it is certain to externalize itself as an objective fact, because your will acts upon the unformed creative, or primary, Intelligence, and causes it to take the form that you have determined upon.

PUPIL: That does not sound so difficult. Of one thing I am certain, that is, that my entire environment is the result of my habitual tendency of thought. Also, that when I know that I should turn my thoughts into other channels, but do not, simply letting them run along the lines of least resistance, it is because my will is weak and untrained. Will you please tell me the quickest way that this can be remedied?

YOU ACQUIRE ENERGY, AS WELL AS AMBITION,
BY EXERCISING THE WILL

SAGE: I will give you a few exercises for developing the will, and from these you can fashion others to suit your own requirements. In the first place, it is important to realize that any tendency to strain will be detrimental and must be avoided. Such exercises are not only interesting, but stimulating, and if persistently practiced will keep your ambitions from lagging. They will give you new impulses, renewed energy, and determination to be and to do something better and greater than anything in the past. Once you are fully conscious of the place and power of your will, in the mental realm, to keep the creative energy at work in formulating your desires, you will realize that it is very susceptible to training, and you will never again be content to live without its constant use, for it would be like living only half a life.

PUPIL: May I ask a question right here? I am a fairly good pianist but dislike to begin my practice, and, although I enjoy it once I have begun, to start is always a struggle. If I were to compel myself to practice on the piano at a certain time every day, would that develop and strengthen my will?

SAGE: It would help, but the greatest benefit would be in the direction of making you a better musician. The best way to strengthen your will is to practice exercises for the sole purpose of strengthening the will, always remembering, while taking them, that your effort is for self-training and self-control, to the end that you many realize yourself as a part of the great universal whole. In this way you gain a peaceful centralization, which, though maintained by a conscious act of the will, is the very essence of rest. With a well-developed, trained will, your thoughts will never wander from the consciousness that "all is life, and all is good, and nature, from her clearly visible surface to her most arcane depths, is a storehouse for good."

You have the key to her great treasures, and whatever appeals to you most at any particular time and place, is that mode of the universal Living Spirit with which you are at that moment most in touch. Realizing this, you draw from out the universe streams of vital energy, which make the very act of living a joy, which radiate from you vibrations that can turn aside all injurious suggestions. *This* is surely a good and sufficient reason for developing the will.

EXERCISE FOR STRENGTHENING THE WILL

The will is weak because of lack of exercise. Training the will is very much the same as training the muscles. Its development is gradual. Only will can develop will; consequently, you begin with what will you have, and expand and strengthen it through its action upon itself. The weak will manifests in two phases: over-action and under-action; the former as impulsiveness, impetuousness, and the like, and the latter as lethargy, phlegmatism, etc.

JOE VITALE

It is good to begin each day with a resolution *not to hurry*, and *not to leave* any *task unfinished*. Effort in this direction is of inestimable value. There should be only *one* object in your mind with reference to your exercise — the development and strengthening of your will. At the time have no thought of your improvement as a musician, for if there is any ulterior motive, your will-training will be lost sight of.

CULTIVATE THE FEELING OF CONTENTMENT

Cultivate the sense of contentment, and begin your exercise with that feeling, determining to do it in a happy frame of mind. *This is important.* Take your exercise at the time of day when interruptions are least likely to occur, for seven consecutive days, ten consecutive minutes a day. If an interruption occurs during the exercise, start all over again. If you forget the exercise for one day before you have finished your course of seven days, begin the entire set again and go through with it uninterruptedly.

Place a notebook and pencil by your side before beginning. Now take fifty matches, beads, buttons, bits of paper, or any other small objects, and drop them slowly and deliberately into a box one by one, with a feeling of contentment and satisfaction, declaring with each movement, "*I will to will.*" The one and most important thought is that you are training your will for the particular advantage of having a trained will, and this is why you should cultivate the feeling of contentment. The only method by which you can study the development of your will is by self-analysis and introspection, so, when you have finished your practice, ask yourself such questions as these:

"What did I think about the exercise while I was doing it? Did I believe it would really cultivate my will, or did I do it just because I was told to? Did I actually concentrate on dropping the matches into the box, or was I more concerned with their arrangement, or was I distracted with other thoughts, good or bad? Was I watching the time impatiently, or was I consciously engaging in thoughts of satisfaction and contentment? Did I have a sense of strain, or did it brace me up? Do I believe that it will really train my will if I faithfully follow it up long enough to prove it?" etc., etc.

Write down this series of questions and answers in your notebook. You will find it both interesting and encouraging to keep this record and thus watch your progress.

STIMULATING AN INTEREST IN YOUR WILL EXERCISE

You can stimulate interest in your exercise by varying your resolution or intention. That is, one time hold a conscious attitude of *joyously* willing to will, another of *powerfully* willing to will, another of *peacefully*, and another *contentedly*, etc., etc. These variations in the exercise with the suggestions for introspection, which have been slightly changed, were taken from the best authority, as far as I know, along the lines of will-training, and I am positive will bring the attainment of a firm, strong will, and an intelligent use of it.

LESSON V: MAKING YOUR SUBJECTIVE MIND WORK FOR YOU

"The most potent force in the universe is the influence of the subconscious mind. The proper training of the correlation between the subliminal and the objective faculties is the open sesame that unlocks the richest of all storehouses,—the faculty of *remembering*. And with remembering there follows natural reflections, vision, knowledge, culture, and all that tends to make of man a god, though in the germ."—*Dr. Edwin F. Bowers.*

PUPIL: The subject of the subjective mind greatly interests me. I am sure that had I understood what you have said concerning it, I would have realized that all that was necessary to obtain my desires was to think out exactly what I wanted, consciously place it in my subjective mind, and it would at once begin to attract ways and means for its corresponding physical or material fulfillment.

SAGE: Indeed the study of the subjective mind is an all-absorbing subject. I may be able to enlighten and help you to make working realities out of what now seems to be vague and even mysterious. But it will rest entirely with you to put *vitality* into these suggestions, and that can only be accomplished through using them.

PUPIL: You mean that by making practical use of your suggestions, I will be able to attain practical results which will help not only myself but others also?

SAGE: That is the idea. It has always seemed to me that the average person prefers the satisfaction of giving to another what he requires, rather than helping or teaching him how to attract the desired things to himself, which would give him in addition a feeling of assurance and liberty. You would unquestionably enjoy giving to others, and the recipient would likewise enjoy receiving, but, as a rule, it tends to pauperize the spirit of independence.

PUPIL: If I were to put into my subconscious mind a definite idea that all people have the same power in their subconscious minds to attract to themselves the things they desire through their own efforts, would that thought register in their subconscious minds?

SAGE: That would be the intelligent way of impersonally helping others to connect with their limitless supply.

PUPIL: You have told me before that there was a definite way of impressing the subconscious mind with a particular thought. Would you mind explaining this again?

"GET INTO THE SPIRIT OF YOUR DESIRE"

SAGE: The process is quite different from that of retaining an idea in the so-called intellectual mind. It is necessary, above all else, to *get into the spirit of your desire*, and an effort to feel relaxed and confident will help you to do this. "The spirit of a thing is that which is the source of its inherent movement." For example, if you wish to impress your subconscious mind with the sense of contentment, you must meditate on the quality of contentment. See how that affects you. If in response to your meditation you feel relaxed and confident, you may be sure that your subconscious mind has been impressed with that thought. This is getting "into the spirit" of contentment; not because of certain physical reasons, but because of your recognition of life's action in you in this specific direction. You have the whole of Universal Mind to draw from. There is no limit to the creative power of your subjective mind once you have impressed it with your intention. This example applies to everything great or small.

PUPIL: Since my subjective mind is a part of the Universal Mind, if I impress it with an idea or desire, does this impression pass automatically into the Universal Subjective Mind?

SAGE: Your subjective mind is in essence the same as the Universal Subjective Mind with which it is inseparably connected. It should be understood that your subjective mind receives its impressions from the objective mind and never from material *things*. It is therefore necessary to withdraw your thought from the material or physical *thing* you desire, and to mentally dwell upon the *spiritual symbol* of it, which is the inherent source of its formation.

HOW TO VISUALIZE AND OBJECTIFY THE MENTAL IMAGE

All this may seem somewhat involved to you, because it is the study of the intangible rather than the tangible, but it will unfold to you as we go on, and it will seem quite simple. All we know of the invisible is gained from what we see it do on the plane of the visible. Perhaps an illustration will give you a clearer idea of that interior part of your being, which is the support of all that which must naturally subsist in the universal here and the everlasting now.

First, endeavor to realize yourself as pure spirit, the essential quality of which is good. Pure spirit is pure life, and, naturally, the only thing it could desire is to manifest more and more life, without reference to the forms through which the manifestation takes place. Consequently, "the purer your intention, the more readily it is placed in your subconscious mind," which instantly passes it into the Universal Mind.

For example: If you want a house, a certain kind of a chair, a sum of money, or anything else, you should first ponder studiously on how the desired object originated. Meditating thus on the original spirit of the thing in question starts the creative power of your subjective mind (which is in touch with all the creative energy which exists) operating in that specific direction.

Suppose it is a house you desire. You will go back to the original concept of it. The idea of a house had its origin in a primary need for shelter, protection from the elements, and comfort, and out of these original desires there grew our present dwellings. So you proceed to build a house in your own consciousness first, thinking only harmonious, constructive thoughts regarding it. This kind of thinking (or building) gives your subjective mind definite material to work with, and because of its amenableness to suggestion, coupled with its native creative power, it will go ahead and eventually bring the hose into manifestation.

PUPIL: If I earnestly and righteously desire a certain kind of a home, how shall I proceed?

PROJECT THE PICTURE OF YOUR HOUSE

SAGE: You should first form a clear conception in your objective mind of the sort of a house which you desire; whether one, two, or three stories; the number and size of the rooms; how many windows and doors; in short, you should mentally picture the completed house, both inside and out. Go all around the house; look over the exterior; then go indoors and examine it carefully from cellar to garret in every detail. Then drop the picture and dwell in the spiritual prototype of the house.

PUPIL: I do not fully understand what the spiritual prototype is.

SAGE: The simplest method of finding a spiritual prototype of any object is to ask yourself to what use it is to be put, what does it stand for, in other words, what is the reason for its being? As we have been saying, a house is a place of shelter, comfort, protection. It might be called a refuge.

PUPIL: Then if I want a house (really a home), and there seems no ordinary way of my having it, I am to impress my desire upon by subjective mind, by mentally picturing the type of house I want, in conjunction with the ideas of shelter, comfort, and protection, and mentally live in that state of mind, while, in order to supplement a mental atmosphere of "pure intention," I admit no thoughts of discord, such as anger, jealousy, doubt, fear, etc., but entertain thoughts of love, joy, beauty, and harmony. Would this not be literally living in my true mental abode? And could I not expect to see it objectified in a material home?

WHAT THE HOUSE SYMBOLIZES

SAGE: Yes, because every physical or material thing is the *result* of an idea first possessed in consciousness. These ideas, which are universal by nature, are specialized by your mental picture, and your concentrated effort to inhibit thoughts which concern the operation of the laws of life. This habit of thought-formation, if persisted in, opens the way for the physical manifestation of the mental picture, whatever it may be, the case in point being a house. A house is an effect of a need for shelter, comfort, protection, and the life.

PUPIL: I have never thought before of what a house really symbolized. It seems quite natural now to think of it as an externalized object of an inward originating idea of comfort, shelter, and protection, which you have taught me is its prototype. Now, my natural impulse would be to go into the house and bolt the doors and windows, if I were afraid of some outside invasion and wanted to protect myself. Yet this might not always give me a feeling of security. From where does that sense of real protection come?

LIVING IN THE SENSE OF PROTECTION

SAGE: The first necessity would be for you to have the house to go into, before you could bolt the doors and windows against unwelcome intrusion or impending danger. After having acquired this refuge, it alone would not insure complete protection. The feeling of protection is established within yourself through your knowledge that you are protected by the Almighty, Ever-Present, Intelligent Power of Life. Surely you know you are alive, and this understanding brings a sense of security which locked doors or barred windows cannot give.

PUPIL: It would be wonderful if one could constantly live in that thought of protection!

SAGE: It is to this end we are journeying. As we have seen, in the mind of man there is a power which enables him to contact the unlimited universal Power of God, Spirit, and thereby envelop himself in it. One of the most satisfying and comforting feelings possible is this one of being protected from within oneself.

PUPIL: I see. One should endeavor to keep the suggestion of one's real self, which is one's real protection, constantly in mind; that self which is one with all Life and all Intelligence, which not only preserves but provides for all.

To return to the subject of the house. It being, then, the outward fulfillment or manifestation of a desire or need for shelter and protection, the mode of procedure necessary to procure it would be to get into the spirit of Life's intelligent protection, and it in turn would attract the necessary conditions to bring into tangible being a house, or whatever form of refuge was most required, and visualized?

SAGE: Mentally entering into the spirit of Life's amenable creative force, it will take any special form your desire gives it, which is mentally pictured or visualized. The house is only an illustration.

PUPIL: I understand. Now suppose one wanted more money or better health. What would be the prototype for these?

SAGE: It is always best to find one's own prototype. Let us refer to the suggestions I have already given you. What does money symbolize? For what is it to be used? For myself, I find that the prototype for money is Substance, and my method for manifesting more money is to mentally picture the sum I require for a particular purpose, either in bank-notes, check, or draft, whichever seems the most natural. After making a clear, distinct picture, I enlarge my vision of money as the symbol of life's substance, as applied to the use I intend to put it to. I believe that money is the greatest factor for constructive exchange that we have today.

HOW TO DEVELOP HEALTH AND HARMONY

In the case of money, you would hold firmly in your mind the fact that the Substance of Life fills all space. It is, indeed, the starting point of all things, whether it takes the form of desired sums of money or of something else.

For physical health you would endeavor to keep your thought as harmonious as possible, and mentally picture yourself as well and doing the useful, happy things in your daily life that a healthy person would naturally do, always understanding that the originating Life Principle in you must act harmoniously upon itself in order to produce harmonious physical results.

PUPIL: Then the most important point in demonstrating health is not so much the mental picture, as the control of thought in a definite center, irrespective of conditions or symptoms—really living in the prototype, a wholly perfect and harmonious expression of God the Father Spirit, the source of health and life?

SAGE: Exactly, and this is where your trained will comes in to help you to *hold your picture* and to steadfastly *live in your prototype*. The mental picture is the seed you plant, so to speak, and the quality of thought which you entertain most persistently impresses itself upon the subconscious mind and starts the creative energy moulding itself into the form of your mental picture.

PUPIL: Then Life's only creative power is Subjective Mind, which reproduces on the outward or physical plane the idea with which it has been impressed. What a field of possibilities this stupendous fact opens up if one could only prove it!

SAGE: To obtain continuous good results it is a necessity to *properly understand your relation* to this great unformed, highly impressionable power you are dealing with. "Never try to make yourself believe what you know is not true." Unless your faith is built upon the solid foundation of absolute conviction, you will never be able to make practical use of it.

PUPIL: This solid foundation of conviction,—how can it be established permanently? One day I feel sure of it, and the next my assurance seems to have turned to stone, and nothing I can do will bring it to life again!

USE YOUR CREATIVE POWER CONSTRUCTIVELY,
NEVER DESTRUCTIVELY

SAGE: You give your unqualified consent that you possess this creative power when you use it constructively instead of destructively. Remember, that the creative energy has only one method of operating, which is its reciprocal action from the Universal Mind to your subjective mind, and then from your subjective mind back into the Universal Subjective Mind which is its source, and which unfailingly corresponds to the thought which originally generated it. Your greatest aim should be to irrevocably convince yourself that the Originating Spirit which brought the whole world into existence is the root of your individuality. Therefore, it is "ever ready to continue its creative action through you." *Just as soon and just as fast as you provide these thought channels, you will find yourself the possessor of an unfailing reproductive power.*

PUPIL: I suppose I am not unlike others, in that I am always willing to take all the credit for the good which comes to me, and unwilling to take the credit for my miseries, placing the blame on somebody or some condition over which I believe I have no control. How can I overcome this wretched tendency?

SAGE: I can only repeat, by endeavoring steadfastly to remember that the only creative power there is has but one way of working, which is that of reciprocal action. There is only one primary cause; the Universal Subjective Mind, of which your own subjective mind is a part. To gain in understanding, it is necessary to be persistent in impressing your subconscious mind with the fact of its relationship to the unlimited whole. Bring your every thought and feeling into obedient connection with the best there is in you. This old saying has a world of truth in it: "What thou see'st, that thou be'st; dust if thou see'st dust; God if thou see'st God."

HOLD THE THOUGHT OF WHAT YOU ARE, TO GUIDE YOU INTO WHAT YOU WANT TO BE.

PUPIL: Which means, I suppose, that the law is always the same. The thought I maintain becomes a fact in my mental as well as in my physical plane, so I must hold the thought of *what I really am* in order to become what I would like to be?

SAGE: Yes, endeavor *never* to lose sight of this fact.

PUPIL: Like the illustration you gave of the house, it has its birth in the idea of protection, irrespective of any physical form?

SAGE: Protection is an inherent quality of life; consequently it fills all space, ever ready to be called into any form of expression. If you get into the spirit of that idea, you will see how quickly corresponding results will appear. Because the quality of the subjective mind is the same in you as it is "throughout the universe, giving rise to the multitude of natural forms with which you are surrounded, also giving rise to yourself," it really is the supporter of your individuality. Your individual subjective mind is your part in the great whole, as I have declared before. The realization of this will enable you to produce physical results through the power of your own thought.

PUPIL: That reveals to me your meaning in "The Edinburgh Lectures," page 33, where you say, "One should regard his individual subjective mind as the organ of the absolute, and his objective mind as the organ of the relative." I will never forget that fact again.

CULTIVATE THE IDEA OF PROTECTION

SAGE: The idea in the absolute is the very beginning (or nucleus) of the thing, regardless of the form through which it expresses. For instance, the pure idea of protection exists in life itself (is one of its innate qualities) and has no relation to a house or any building erected for that purpose.

PUPIL: Then it is my objective mind or intellect which suggests to this self-existing, absolute power the idea of this relationship?

SAGE: Quite so, and if you will pattern the thought you have just expressed, telling your subconscious mind over and over again that it is the one and only creative power, which always brings into physical manifestation corresponding forms of the ideas with which it is impressed, you will realize the joys of success.

PUPIL: I "see through a glass darkly."   Is there no way to develop a keener sense of just how to awaken the subconscious mind so that it will respond more quickly?

SAGE: I will be happy to give you a copy of a letter I once wrote in response to a question similar to yours. This letter was considered so helpful that the men to whom it was written had it put into pamphlet form, now out of print. It seems to me that the main thing that I said in that letter was "Don't try!"

PUPIL: Why! I thought that trying was to be my main endeavor, even though it was difficult!

A LETTER OF GOLDEN LEAVES

The Sage's Letter

"To answer your question as to how a 'Keener sense of the subjective mind may be awakened," the answer is 'Don't try. Don't try to make thing what they are not.' Subjective mind is subjective just because it lies below the threshold of consciousness. It is the Builder of the Body, but we can neither see, hear, nor feel it building.

Just keep in your conscious mind a quiet, calm expectation that subjective mind is always at work in accordance with the habitual thought of your objective mind . . . and then subjective mind will take care of itself.

Then the question is, how to keep the conscious thought in a life-enjoying and life-giving current. My answer to this is very simple, though perhaps old--fashioned. It is, keep looking at God. Don't trouble about theology, but try to realize the Universal Divine Spirit as perpetually flowing through all things; through insensible things as atomic energy; through animals as instinct; through man as thought.

If this be so, then your manifestation of God will correspond with your habitual thought of God. Quietly contemplate the Divine Spirit as a continual flowing of Life, Light, Intelligence, Love and Power, and you will find this current flowing through you and manifesting in a hundred ways, both mentally and physically, in your affairs.

You do not make this current, but you prepare the conditions which will either cause it to trickle through thinly and weakly, or flow through strongly. You prepare the conditions on the interior side by a mental attitude of looking into the light (God is Light) with the expectancy of thence receiving life and Illumination, and on the exterior side by not denying in your work what you are trying to hold in your thought,—for yourself the simple Law of Enjoyment of all that you can enjoy, ruled by moderation, and toward others the equally simple Law of Honesty and Kindness.

I know you have heard these things ever since you were a child, but what we all want is to realize our connection with the building power within. The connection is this: that the Spirit, as it flows through you, becomes you, and it becomes in you just what you take it for, just as water takes the shape of the pipe it flows through. It takes shape from your thought. It is exceedingly sensitive—how much more, then, must the pure Life Principle itself be sensitive? Think over this. Think it over and then think. Think of it kindly, lovingly, trustfully, and as a welcome companion. It will respond exactly. Think of it as a Living Light, continually flowing through and vivifying you, and it will respond exactly.

If you ask why it does this, the answer is because IT is the Infinite of your Real Self. Let this answer suffice you. You will only darken the Light by trying to analyze the Divine Spirit. You cannot dissect God. This doesn't mean being impractical, but getting to the very root of truly practical. We have our ordinary business to do, but, believe me, it is the scientific method to bring everything into the Divine Light.

Then let your ideas be desires to see it in the Divine Light, let your ideas regarding it grow quietly of themselves, and you will see it in its proper and true light whatever the thing may be. Then when you have seen what the thing really is, go on and handle it in accordance with the four principles of Cheerfulness, Moderation, Honestly and Kindness. Don't worry, and don't try to force things; let them grow, because, by recognizing the continual flow of the Spirit, you are providing the conditions, for Life is the Light which will make them grow the right way.

Don't bother about subjective mind and objective mind, or theories of any sort, or description, either mine or anyone else's; but just do what I have said and try it for six months, and I think you will find you have got hold of the Power that Works, and, after all, that is what we want.

It is all summed up in this: Live naturally with the Spirit and don't worry. Remember, you and your Spirit are One, and it is all quite natural. You will perhaps say that this is too simple. Well, we don't want to introduce unnecessary complications. Try practicing and leave the theory to take care of itself. Living Spirit is not to be found in a book."

SAGE: Many have written me from all parts of the world voicing your expression. Once a lady in New York City wrote asking me to explain to her exactly what I mean in the pamphlet about Spirit becoming you. Thinking you might like to see a copy of my reply, I brought it along for you.

PUPIL: Thank you so much. Am I at liberty to keep these letters?

SAGE: Quite.

THE LETTER OF THE MASTER

"With regard to the sentence in the pamphlet on the Subjective Mind about the Spirit *becoming* you, I really don't see how to express my meaning any more clearly. What I mean is that in a cat it becomes a cat; and in a cabbage it becomes a cabbage; but in man, who is conscious, living intelligence, it becomes conscious, living intelligence. And if so, then, since the *Spirit* is *Infinite* you can by prayer and meditation draw upon it for increased living intelligence, i.e., all depends on your mode of recognition of it.

In the sentence you quote, 'It is exceedingly sensitive,' etc. , I am not referring to the water, but the Spirit. I mean that if subconscious mind in ourselves is sensitive to suggestion, the creative principle is sensitive to suggestion, the creative principle from which it springs must be still more so, and takes shape from your thought accordingly. But you must remember that the pamphlet was not written for publication. It was merely a private letter, and I was never consulted on the subject of publishing it, or perhaps I should have worded it more carefully.

Supply and demand is a very large subject, but eventually you will always have to come back to the teaching of Jesus, 'Ask and ye shall receive.' We may write volumes on the subject, but in the end it always comes to this, and we have gained nothing by going a long way around. I am coming more and more to see that the teaching of Jesus is the final embodiment of all that writers on those subjects are trying to teach. In the end we have to drop all our paraphernalia of argument and come back to His statement of the working method. All the Bible promises are based on the divine knowledge of your mental constitution, and by simple reliance on it we therefore afford centers through which the Creative Power of the Universe can act in correspondence with our recognition of it. 'According to your faith so be it unto you.' Our faith is our *real thought*. If our real thought is expectation of disease and poverty, *that* is our faith—and we have faith in this power of disease, and so open the door to it. The whole purpose of the Bible is to direct our thought (which is our faith) in the right way, instead of leaving us to form it invertedly. Therefore, as the basis for our faith, the Bible gives us *Promises*. Pin your faith to the Promises, and you need not bother your brains to argue about it. The more you argue, the more you will pin your faith to your own argument and your understanding of the law; and as a logical sequence you make the fulfillment of your desire depend on your correct arguing and exact knowledge, so that the result is you are depending *entirely upon yourself*—and so you are 'no forwarder' and are just where you were.

On the other hand by simply believing the Divine Promises, you transfer the whole operation to the Divine Spirit (your subjective mind), and so you have a good ground of expectation, and by your mental *receptive* attitude you become a 'fellow worker' with God. You *allow* the All Creating Spirit to work in, for, and through you. This is the conception St. Paul always had in his epistles, in all of them showing the weakness of relying on Law, and the strength of Faith in Promises. This also, I think, was Jesus' meaning when He said: 'Blessed is he that hath not seen and yet hath believed.' Well, I hope that these few remarks will be useful to you, but I am wondering how this point of view will appeal to an American audience, and that is another reason why I am rather doubtful about coming over. The more I think on this subject, the less I see in trying to make 'Supply,'

'Health,' and all the usual New Thought topics the subject of a set of mechanical rules like the rules of arithmetic. It throws the burden back on yourself, while your whole object is to get rid of it. It is the old temptation of Eden over again—the Tree of Knowledge, reliance on our own acquisition of Knowledge; on the Tree of Life,—reliance on God's own nature and His desire for expression *in* us and *through* us, which is the meaning of all the promises. The former *looks clever* but isn't. The latter *looks childish* but is the *fulfillment* of *all law*, and is *life*.

If you see things in this light, which I am sure is the true one, the model you will have to take for the 'School of the Builders' is 'The stone which the builders rejected has become the head of the corner.' The reference is to the great pyramid and the topmost stone—also to our crowning stone in Westminster Abbey—and of course it refers superlatively to Christ. But properly instructed builders do not reject this stone. On the contrary, they recognize it as both the Foundation and the Apex of the Building of the Temple. You remember how St. Paul calls himself a wise master-builder.

Is it any use for me to come to America to teach these things, which is some form or another have been taught there ever since the arrival of the *Mayflower*? Of course, I can talk about *Vibration, Nervous System*, the *Pyramid*, and the like, and the working of *Natural Laws*; but the Creating Principle is apart. 'A worshipper of God and a student of Nature' is what one of our old thinkers called himself. The *Power* is *of God* and is *received* by Man and Man exercises it *upon* nature. That is the true order.

One meaning of the Masonic symbol of the five-pointed star is that everything returns to its starting point. Start from the apex of the triangle and trace the line around and you come back to the apex. If, then, your starting point is in Heaven, you go back to Heaven and the Divine Power, and so get rid of the burden; but if your starting point is on earth (i.e., your own acquisition of knowledge of laws), you get back to earth, which is indicated by the inverted triangle.

You will find the Promises of man's power over Nature, Conditions, etc., fully stated in Mark 11:22-25, and no teaching can promise more than this."

GOD HAS RIPENED A GREAT MIND

PUPIL: No words can express what a privilege I feel it to have you thus unfold and make clear to me the truths I have struggled so hard to understand. God has surely blessed you with one of the greatest minds of the present generation.

SAGE: Not at all. There are many who know much more than I along these lines. For myself, however, I am certain that there is but one God, that *God and man are one*, and that my mind is a center of Divine Operation; this in itself is a blessing. Much has already been written on these subjects; it is all so simple.

PUPIL: I know it is simple to you, but to us, who are struggling between certainty and uncertainty, it is a rare benefit to be able to sit and listen at the feet of *certainty*.

SAGE: I am happy indeed that these lessons have been helpful. It has been a great pleasure for me to have exchanged ideas with you, and I know that you will pass them on to others whenever you feel they will be helpful. It seems to me that you now have all the material necessary to build for yourself a foundation and superstructure of absolute faith in God and of the *power of God in you*, which is your subjective mind. This knowledge, *well established*, gives you dominion over every adverse circumstance and condition, because you are in conscious touch with your limitless supply. "Only believe in the God within, and all things are possible unto you."

LESSON VI: HOURLY HELPS

SAGE: I want in this lesson to give you, in the most practical form, the means whereby you may meet the disquieting things of life—the things which wear soul, spirit, and body almost to the snapping point. I want you to take these admonitions and instructions into your most intimate life and keep them bright and shining by daily use. They will help you hourly in overcoming destructive elements, and in attracting constructive ones.

Anger

When anger begins to stir you, take deep breaths; hold your thought on the inflow of breath as being rays of light, breathing deeper and deeper. Continue the deep breaths until you have taken twenty-five inhalations; hold each one while you count to seven. Then expel slowly, keeping your thought steadily on the inhalation, mentally seeing it go all through your lungs, and penetrating every part of your body as rays of light. Then meditate upon any real live thought about yourself, such as being *one with all life and good*. A little practice in this way will soon relieve you of the tendency to anger.

Anxiety

When conditions are not to your liking and you find yourself thinking more and more about how unhappy you are because of them, stay out of doors in the open all you possibly can. Endeavor to walk at least two miles every day, breathing deeply of the fresh air with this thought: "I am breathing in the Life, the Love and the Power of the universe, *right now*." Do not permit your thought to slip back into the old groove. Fill your mind with this declaration about yourself. You have been given dominion over every adverse condition through your power of thought. Persist in your steady recognition of this fact. Tell yourself over and over again that all is well right now in your thought and feeling; consequently outside conditions *must and will* correspond.

Disease

If your body is the expression of thought, then disease must be the result of a belief that your body is subject to disease. Tell yourself many times a day that all physical disease is the result of discordant thoughts, and when you have actually accepted this statement as a truth, you will be careful to entertain only healthy, harmonious thoughts for yourself or another. For example, if you feel a headache coming on, begin at once to take deep breaths, and repeat with each breath that breath is Life, and that life is perfect health. "I am alive, so the health of life is manifesting in me right now."

Disappointment

This subtle destructive power should be shut out at all times by the recognition of your direct contact with all the joy there is, because you are one with its Source, Universal Good. If the joyous life does not express itself through the exact channels which you expect, know that it will do so through others. Life wants to express joy through you, for it made you an instrument in which and through which to do it. Because you are here for that purpose, you can and do enjoy all the good which Life has to give. Take some physical exercises while holding that thought. A good one is to sit on a chair and take a deep breath; then slowly exhale, and as you exhale, gradually bend at the hips until you can touch the floor with the tips of your fingers. Repeat this seven times with the affirmation: "The joy of God is flowing in me and through me right now."

Discontent

When this enemy to peace and happiness begins to advance, sing, sing sing, right out loud if you can, or else do it mentally. Sing anything you like. Watch your breath control, and every night put into your subconscious mind the thought that God brought you into existence for the purpose of expressing all of Life's harmonies, both in you and through you, and it is your divine right to BE harmony and to be harmonious in your daily experience. Meditate upon the harmony you see expressed in nature and endeavor to apply it in your thought, and then *express* it.

Discouragement

This is failure on your part to recognize the Almighty limitless Source of Supply (God) as your never-failing, co-operative partner. When you are assailed with the thought of discouragement, immediately ask yourself, "What kind of a power was it that brought me into existence, and for what purpose?" Then repeat slowly and *thinkingly*, "I do believe and I am persuaded that God is an ever-present, never-failing source of protection and supply." Watch your thoughts lest any contrary to this affirmation be lurking around in the corners of your mind, and *stick to it* with all the will that you have, and you will break down the suggestion that there is any power in discouragement.

Envy

Envy is due to a sense of separation from God, Good. Endeavor to realize that where there is life, all that life has to give is present in its entirety at all times and in all places, and will come into visible expression through the persistent recognition of this grand fact.

Fear

One writer has said that fear is the only devil there is. Certainly it is the most destructive power one can entertain. When fear comes to assail you, close the door of your mind against it with this positive thought: "The only creative power there is, is thought. All things are possible to him who believes that the God which brought man into existence did so for the purpose of expressing His Fatherly love and protection in His child. I believe in God, the Father Almighty, as my life, my intelligence, manifesting in my consciousness *now*." As you think this, walk briskly or take strenuous exercise. Whenever you sense fear returning, inhibit it instantly by substituting any thought which *affirms the power of God in you*. In short, fear is absolutely overcome by withdrawing your thought from the physical reason or argument which would cause you to believe in a power other than God, and the spirit of Life and Love as your birthright.

Indecision

This is a lack of the realization that your intelligence is the instrument through which the Intelligence of the universe takes specific form. An effort to realize this fact should be a habit of mind, rather than spasmodic attempts made only when the necessity for decision arises.

Jealousy

This is love's greatest enemy, and if permitted to dwell within your consciousness, will ultimately destroy your ability to enjoy your life. It is the reaction of the fear of loss and can be overcome through prayer and watchfulness. Reason along these lines: "God is Life and God is Love. I am life and I am love. I cannot lose Love any more than I can lose Life."   When you are tempted to feel jealous, walk long distances as frequently as possible and keep your thought on Love itself, not on any one person whom you love, but just Love and its attributes.   Think of God as Love. Keep all thought of personality out of mind, and you will find that love will spring up in you as a fountain of everlasting love and life and fill your consciousness through and through.

Self-Condemnation

The instant you begin to blame yourself to having done the wrong thing or for not having done the right thing, put this thought into your consciousness to the exclusion of every other: "Infinite Intelligence and Wisdom are expressing themselves in me more and more right now." Take the exercise of bending the body from the hips (without bending the knees) so that you can touch the floor with the tips of your fingers, inhaling as you lift the body, and exhaling every time you bend. Repeat this exercise sixteen times, accompanied by the affirmation just given.

Self-Indulgence

This is brought about by lack of will-power: an evidence of a weak will. It means failure, because you have no thought-power to give the unformed energy of life the particular thought-material necessary to produce desired results. Absolute mental (thought) control is the one and only thing which is necessary for you to do, to be, or to have what you want. Without it, you scatter your forces.

If you permit your thoughts to run riot without restraint, the conditions of your life will become chaotic. For example: A friend does something of which you do not approve, or perhaps your present circumstances are undesirable. Refuse to let your thought dwell on the injustice of your friend, for dwelling on it would only produce greater unhappiness for you. Control your thought and do not think of your friend in this connection. Instead, consider the many fine attributes of friendship, and this will restore harmony. Do the same in regard to your unpleasant circumstances. Don't picture them mentally and say to yourself, "How dreadful they are!" But repeat the glorious truth which I have previously referred to: "My mind is a center of divine operation," etc., and divine operation is always for greater advancement and better things. You will experience this if you cling faithfully to this line of reasoning.

Sensitiveness

A highly sensitive mind is simply a "self-mind," a form of unadulterated selfishness. Your feelings are hurt because someone says something which *you* do not like, or does something which displeases *you*. Or conversely, he fails to say or to do what *you* think he should. To eradicate this baneful thought-habit, use the same method of argument as for self-indulgence, and if faithful in your mental work, your efforts will be rewarded, and you will free yourself.

Unhappiness

A continually unhappy state of mind is the direct result of constantly viewing life from the physical standpoint as though that were life's only reality. Every night, before you go to sleep, put well into your subconscious mind this thought: "There is but One Mind to think about me or to make laws over me, and that is the Mind of Divine Love and Divine Power." Every morning meditate upon this thought. Use it as your shield and buckler at the first suggestion of any sense of unhappiness. You will soon find that the tendency to be discontented and unhappy will vanish, and happier conditions will come into your experience.

LESSON VII: PUTTING YOUR LESSONS INTO PRACTICE

Just as I am completing this manuscript for the printer, the idea suggests *itself* that it will also be helpful to give a definite idea, in formula form, of how to be and have what you want.

First, you should endeavor to learn to be as near the perfect reflection of your own idea of God as possible, in thought and action. It may seem impossible at first thought, to even approach such a goal, but reflection upon the thought that God made you out of Himself, because He wished to see and feel Himself in you, will help you to persevere. When you first began to learn to read, no doubt you felt in your childish way that it would be wonderful to read as well as the grown-ups could; you *kept on trying and then you read*.

Perhaps you have a big desire which you would give your life to have fulfilled. In reality it is only necessary for you to give a few moments each day to earnest effort, in getting into the spirit of this idea of God and living in it every waking hour. Then endeavor to find the Spiritual Prototype for your desire. By this I mean inhibit all thought of the physical side of your desire.

If you desire a true companion, close your mind entirely to all personality and physical being, and dwell in thought and feeling on the spirit of love and true comradeship, without reference to any physical person. The person is the instrument through which these particular qualities manifest, and not the qualities themselves, as we often learn too late.

Or you may desire improved financial condition. Here again it is not mere money you desire. It is that which money symbolizes—Substance, Liberty, Freedom from lack. Therefore, you should go alone night and morning (or any time when you are certain you will not be disturbed) and meditate first upon your own true relation to God. After your feeling has been stimulated to the point of certainty, then meditate upon the ever-present, never-failing substance and freedom of God. Try not to lose sight of the fact that the greatest magnet for acquiring money is Ideas. There is every reason that you should capture one of these big money ideas, if you will persistently follow the suggestions given.

If you do this, you will not only capture the idea, but also the courage to put the idea into practical application. This courage, put to positive uses, will bring you to the goal of your desire—substance, love, friends, health, happiness, and the peace that passeth all understanding.

May all these come to you in richest measure.

Hypnotic Marketing Library Collection from Joe Vitale

"These are the secrets you need if you want to create marketing messages (ads, articles, sales letters, emails etc.) that make your prospects stand up and take action...

"Who Else Wants To Learn A Simple, Step-By-Step 'System' For Crafting <u>Hypnotic Marketing Messages</u> That Practically Force YOUR Prospects To Whip Out Their Plastic - Every Time?

"If You Seriously Want To Take Your Business To The NEXT Level... Read Every Word On This Page and Find Out How YOU Can Apply These 'Time-Tested' and *Proven Marketing <u>Secrets</u>* Into YOUR Business..."

Are you serious about your Internet marketing success? Do you want to achieve results in your business that you know you're capable of, but have eluded you until now?

Joe Vitale is **the real deal.** His **Hypnotic Marketing** techniques have created amazing results for Joe and his clients, and now you can take advantage of his incredible knowledge with the **Hypnotic Marketing Library Super Package CD-ROM.** And, you can shave $224 off the price of Joe's complete hypnotic marketing collection when you **take advantage of this special collection price** now.

Over the years, Joe has built quite a reputation for his marketing prowess. If you wanted to hire Joe to just give you some advice, you would pay $500 an hour. Want Joe Vitale to write you a sales letter? It would cost you $12,500 and up. How about a web site critique? This would cost you $650 to start.

If this sounds a little steep, it's not. Joe charges this much because he's worth it. Joe has tons of happy clients who know he's **worth every single penny** they shell out because Joe's marketing techniques and advice always create a **huge return on their investment.** Just look at what some of the top marketers on the Internet are saying about Joe:

"If you can't pull a $50,000 idea out of this e-book you'd better put a mirror to your face and see if it fogs ups. Joe pounds and blitzes you with one incredible idea, story and example after another. My brain was on overload! I give it an A+."

—Yanik Silver, SurefireMarketing.com

"Joe Vitale hypnotized me today! He did it with 'Hypnotic Marketing,' which I found impossible to stop reading. I learned something new on every page, and I've been learning about marketing since 1958. Now, I can only shudder for those poor souls who haven't yet learned what Joe has to teach. Not only does he enlighten, but he does it in such a warm and engaging way, that you cannot help but   complete his book with a smile in your heart and dollar signs on your mind. Thank you, Joe, for a mighty contribution to the world of marketing."

—Jay Conrad Levinson, author
Guerrilla Marketing series

"Joe, you've written a masterpiece. Condensing the formula for getting rich in only 79 days into three simple steps anyone can follow is brilliant! As with everything you write, 'Hypnotic Marketing' is crammed full of true-to-life, straight forward ways to start a welcome flow of cash into anyone's bank account. We all thank you for making this gem available. But, come on, Joe... that price. You've got to be kidding! Why would you give away so much for so little? It's like selling Fort Knox at a discount!"

—Dr. Paul Hartunian
How to Get a Million
Dollars in Publicity FREE!

"Do what 'Hypnotic Marketing' says and you will get rich! It's simply brilliant! I learn something that increases my bottom line profits every time I read Joe Vitale. 'Hypnotic Marketing' is an ENCYCLOPEDIA of specific laser beam strategies of how to market your business NOW. Trust me. I know. The last time I used just ONE of Joe Vitale's ideas in a marketing plan I earned $12,865 in one DAY! (That's just one idea!)"

—Kevin Hogan, Author,
The Psychology of Persuasion

"I finished reading 'Hypnotic Marketing' last night and I just have one question: Pardon my French, Joe, but Jesus Christ, do you have ANY secrets left? I've never seen anybody reveal as many of their secrets in one fell swoop as you did in this book. The only way you could put money in your readers' pockets any faster is if you wrote them a check yourself! My favorite chapter is number 29 on Gold Mine.net. The before and after illustration is dramatic to say the least. Your revised copy is awesome, but when you compare it against the original it is even more so. Also, I really liked your muscle test section. It's a new and fascinating idea. Maybe you'll start a new trend with this one!"

—Blair Warren, Author
The Forbidden Keys to Persuasion

"Awesome! Joe's new book lays out a complete, navigable road map for the marketing novice and veteran alike. You'll find loads of valuable information and specific techniques here. Plus, there are several gems in this book -- like the 5 ways to get people to open an email, and the 5 ways to start a killer email sales letter -- that is each worth at least 10 times the price of the book itself.

Unless you are a billionaire whose only problem is that you have too much money, you need this book!"

—David Garfinkel, Author
Advertising Headlines That Make You Rich

But, thanks to Nitro Marketing, you don't have to shell out the big bucks to get the inside scoop on Joe's Hypnotic Marketing techniques.

Working with Joe, we've created the ultimate Hypnotic Marketing resource -- the **Hypnotic Marketing Library Super Package.**

We've crammed **ten of Joe's best Hypnotic ebooks onto a single CD-ROM**, giving you access to some of the best marketing and copywriting resources that have been produced in the last century. If you had to purchase all 10 of these great products separately, you would have to pay $620.

But because we were able to convince Joe to work with us on this Package, we were able to "twist his arm" and get him to allow us to offer all 10 of these great ebooks on a single CD-ROM for the **incredible price of only $397** (plus s/h). That's a **whopping 40% savings.**

Let's take a small peek into exactly what you will be learning when you take advantage of this very special offer today...

The Hypnotic Marketing Library Super Package

Here's what you'll receive when you order Joe Vitale's Hypnotic Marketing Library Super Package on CD-ROM:

☑ **Hypnotic Writing and Advanced Hypnotic Writing**

Joe shares with you all of the powerful secrets to crafting hypnotic sales materials and also teaches you advanced persuasion techniques that have earned him and his students millions of dollars **(Value: $37 + $67)**

Here's a small sample of what you will learn...

- Learn the top hypnotic secrets that master hypnotists have been **jealously guarding** – which **empower** you to get all the orders you desire from your customers

- How to easily lead your prospect into a hypnotic state, and **program** him to be receptive to your offer – without his realizing you're doing it

- How to skillfully enter the **hypnotic threshold** of your prospects' minds so that they will accept, act upon, and *obey your commands*

- The top 3 things you must do to satisfy a **primal** need that lies deep within your prospects – and make them want to buy whatever you're selling

- How to **secretly** penetrate your prospect's **subconscious mind** and fill it with your powerful hypnotic suggestions

- How to instill in your prospects a **visceral** need they can feel at the **gut level** – and create a desire for a resolution that only your product or service can satisfy

- How to dazzle people with hypnotic sales letters that make them follow your commands

- How to use **outrageous** creativity as a hypnotic mechanism to pull in more sales

- Learn the ultimate secret to controlling the **public mind** – is a diabolical principle of **hidden selling** that creates cash automatically outside of human perception

- Hidden commands you can use to make people do your bidding

- **8 hypnotic devices** you can use immediately to get a guaranteed "yes" to your offer

- The 7 deadly things marketers do that make their prospects "snap out" of the hypnotic state and make the sales process grind to a screeching halt

- How to **melt** the resistance of even the most stubborn, prospect. [This slick hypnotic technique moves mountains.]

- Learn the greatest hypnotic secret ever revealed – this is an advertising "formula" that is absolutely indispensable as you embark on your hypnotic marketing expedition

- How to install a *post-hypnotic suggestion* in your readers' brains so that if they can't buy right now, they will be hypnotically compelled to *buy later*

- How to write intriguing headlines that cast a **spell** on your reader

- What to write in your website that makes people want to visit it, talk about it, and then, in the end, **buy whatever you are selling**

- Learn how to **saturate** your writing with intense, emotion-provoking language that sells every time

- Learn the exact words you can use in a sales letter that will make your customers whip out their wallets and buy from you

- How to write **tantalizing** copy that makes your reader's mouth water with anticipation

- Learn the psychological tricks that make your sales letters impossible to ignore

- Discover little-known hypnotic language patterns that literally **dissolve** your prospect's objections

- Get the **Top-Secret** Checklist – Joe Vitale uses this to pre-test the hypnotic quotient of his letters – pure gold!

- How to write a hypnotic headline – in under 15 seconds

- How to craft embedded commands in your writing that make people feel compelled to act now

- How to create **mesmerizing** stories and scenarios that grab the attention of your reader, and hold him captive all the way to the order page

- Discover the little-known **loophole** in the public's mind that allows you to easily engage your prospects hypnotically

- How to drop hypnotic cues in your prospects' subconscious that create an **instinctive** desire for your product or service

- What hypnotic strategies work online, but not offline – and vice versa

- Create your own hypnotic news releases using these proven models

- How to exploit the one proven hypnotic ad format that always works

- How to use **hypnotic suggestion** to compel editors to call within minutes of receiving your press release

- Plus much, much more...

☑ **Hypnotic Marketing**

Marketing techniques on how to make your publicity, emails and websites hypnotic. **(Value: $67)**

The table of contents alone will reflect just how much is in this work...

STEP ONE: HYPNOTIC PUBLICITY

Chapter 2: How to Hypnotize the Masses with "PO" Ideas

Chapter 3: Flying Midgets and the PR Folk Hero

Chapter 4: **Eight Proven Rules** for Getting Publicity

Chapter 5: Pitching a Heavyweight Boxing Champion and His Sausage

Chapter 6: Show Your Bra!

Chapter 7: 21 Ways to Identify Story Ideas About You or Your Business

Chapter 8: Running Water

Chapter 9: Selling Bloody Games

Chapter 10: One of the Easiest Ways in the World to Get Publicity

Chapter 11: How to Install a "Success Wish" in Your Mind

Chapter 12: The Top Three Ways **Guaranteed to ALWAYS Hypnotize** the Media

Chapter 13: 10 Tips on Becoming Newsworthy from a Media Tigress

Chapter 14: The Seven Laws of Baseball's Greatest Publicist

Chapter 15: The Psychology of Hypnotic Publicity

Chapter 16: Edgy Top Secret Ways to Absolutely Nail Media Attention

Chapter 17: How to Get Rich With **P.T. Barnum's Secret**

Chapter 18: The Amazing Breakthrough Formula Called "E-DR Publicity"

Chapter 19: A New Way to Get 30 times More Replies from the Media!

Chapter 20: 14 Instant Ways to Send Out Your News

Chapter 21: Two Words that Can Get You on Virtually Any Radio or TV show (And a Secret Way to Even Get on Oprah)!

STEP TWO: HYPNOTIC WEBSITES

Chapter 22: Your Keys to Hypnotic Websites

Chapter 23: A Master Copywriter Reveals His Inner Secrets

Chapter 24: A Forbidden **Persuasion Master** Reveals His Secrets

Chapter 25: A Practical Mystic Reveals His Website Secrets

Chapter 26: Declan Dunn Shocks Me with His Website Secrets

Chapter 27: What Are the Hardest-Hitting Direct-Selling Websites Online?

Chapter 28: Some Sexy Advice from the World's Greatest Hypnotist

Chapter 29: How to Transform a So-So Website into a Truly Hypnotic Website

Chapter 30: How An "Inspirational Folk Musician" Can Create a Hypnotic Website

Chapter 31: What You Can Learn from This Really Stupid Website

STEP THREE: HYPNOTIC E-MAIL

Chapter 32: The Secret Nobody Wants You to Know About Making Money Online

Chapter 33: How a Famous Street Magician Can Help You Create Hypnotic E-mail

Chapter 34: How to Create E-mails that **Secretly Seduce Your Readers**

Chapter 35: The Five Best Ways to Create Hypnotic Email Openers

Chapter 36: "How Can the Right Question Bring in 317% More Orders?"

Chapter 37: E-mail Sales Letter Samples that are Making Me Rich

Chapter 38: A **Little Known Secret for Doubling Responses** to Your E-Offers

Chapter 39: How to Make Even More Money With This Unusual E-mail Secret

Chapter 40: What are Five Ways to Get People to Open Your E-mail?

Chapter 41: A Truly "Killer" Hypnotic Sales Letter Used Online AND Off

Chapter 42: The World's Most Unusual Way to Strengthen Your Hypnotic Writing

BONUSES:

Bonus #1: How to Create a **Hypnotic** Viral Marketing Campaign

Bonus #2: The 10 Most Dangerous Marketing Books of All Time

Bonus #3: How to Create Your Own Hypnotic Business Cards

Bonus #4: **Dangerous Selling** -- A New Way to Increase Your Profits

Bonus #5: What Bernice Taught Me About Advertising

Bonus #6: How to Create Sales After Creating Relationships

Bonus #7: The **Three Real Secrets** to Success Today

Epilogue: The Hidden Secret to Getting Rich -- *In Only 79 Days*

☑ Hypnotic Writer's Swipe File

Joe Vitale's personal swipe file of over 1550 copywriting gems that have been proven in the trenches. **(Value: $197)**

Previously, only a trusted few had access to and were able to benefit from the Hypnotic Writer's Swipe File -- and now you can too. Here are just a few of the ways you'll benefit:

- 2 irresistible mind-grabbing words that are **the most powerful copywriting words** of all time and should be used repeatedly in your copy to get immediate results.

- 5 hypnotic agreement questions that will **put prospects in a *"yes" trance*** where they will be conditioned to agree with your next statements.

- 31 hypnotic headline words that will get your sales copy read and can drastically increase your sales.

- 178 psychological copy connectors that you can weave into sentences and paragraphs to **compel** readers to take the actions you want.

- 5 hidden commands that are so good, people won't even realize you are **secretly commanding them.**

- 7 "confusers to take control" statements that will confuse readers and allow your hypnotic words to **get past their mental censors.**

- 5 forbidden hypnotic words that will **slip right into your readers' minds** just because they end in "ly."

- 33 subliminal closings/P.S.'s that will *persuade undecided readers* to order your product immediately.

- 163 emotional provoking words that can **trigger your prospects'** emotions and persuade them to buy your product.

- 860 fill-in-the-blank sentence starters that will **reel in your readers** and get them in the proper state of mind to buy your product.

- Insert any of these 11 powerful **embedded commands** into your sentences to compel people to **obey** you. These are so sneaky -- your prospects will never see them coming!

- Dominate your prospect with 13 hypnotic hype action phrases that surround your offer with an **invisible field of magnetism** that very few people can resist.

- Slip these 5 **forbidden** hypnotic words before your command -- and people will feel compelled to do **exactly** what you say.

- Discover 32 camouflaged headline templates that **disguise** your ad as **riveting** editorial content -- thereby skyrocketing the readership of your ad.

- Discover 63 hypnotic opening statements that **take command** of your prospects' mind, put them under your spell -- and keep them tantalized by every word of your sales letter.

- 7 hypnotic devices that make your prospects virtually "dizzy" with information that they have no recourse but to agree with **whatever you propose.**

- 1 simple prefixes that **disguise** your command as a gentle statement -- thereby making it immensely likely that your prospect will follow your hidden command

- 7 "stop commands" that immediately grab your prospect's attention and make him receptive to any hypnotic suggestion you say next.

- 3 hypnotic story-telling methods that mesmerize people -- and lead them to do exactly what you want.

- Countless **specialized communication patterns** that cast a spell on your prospects, and make them want to do whatever you say.

- 41 bullet modifications that elevate **excitement** and **curiosity** -- and make your bullets even more powerful.

- Choose from 22 visual, auditory and kinesthetic phrases that give you the exact language patterns that appeal to any type of prospect.

- 55 "logic generators" give validity to anything you write -- use these words to get people to respect you as an authority or a leader – a person to be listened to, admired and followed.

✍ Hypnotic Selling Tools

Receive 1739 proven to be effective hypnotic words, phrases and sentences you can use today to instantly make your material hypnotic. (**Value: $47**)

Say the following to yourself, out loud: By reading this powerful ebook you will quickly learn:

... *800 hypnotic sentence starters* that will bypass your prospect's conscious mind and **persuade their subconscious mind to order your product.**

... Uncover *440 mesmerizing copy connectors* that will release the floodgates of your prospect's mind and **lead them straight to your order page.**

... Possess *60 subconscious openers* that will **crack open your prospect's subconscious mind** and make them receptive to your suggestions.

... Own *25 seductive story starters* that will **pull your prospects directly into your sales letter.**

... Discover *131 embedded commands and benefits* that will be persuasive and totally invisible to your prospects!

... Know *21 psychic influences that will telepathically penetrate your prospect's mind* over the Internet!

... Hold *19 sensory persuaders* that will **give convincing proof to anything** you write!

... Learn *12 unforeseen closes* that will **mysteriously close each sale** without your prospects realizing it!

... Extract *16 penetrating P.S.'s* that will help **loosen your prospect's mental buying defenses** and give them confidence in purchasing!

... Unearth *160 mind opening questions* that will **automatically unlock your prospect's brain** and trigger persuasive, mental movies!

... Find out *20 unorthodox suggestions* that **will influence your prospect's mind to absorb and believe your information!**

... Use *25 forbidden benefits* that will **condition your prospects to persuade themselves to buy!**

... Master **10 emotional triggers** that will **arouse your prospect's inner buying feelings!**

... And **be gloriously RICH!**

☑ **How to Write Hypnotic Articles**

Shows you how to get free publicity by writing hypnotic articles that people want to publish. **(Value: $37)**

Would you settle for being able to write a hypnotic article in less than 7 minutes? Yes? Well, good, because here's just 17 things you'll learn...

1. The **17 benefits of writing and submitting free reprint articles** to e-zines and Web sites

2. **The secret formula** for writing articles at warp speed

3. How to **quickly and easily roll out** one or two articles every week

4. *30 possible reasons* your article won't get published

5. How to **persuade someone else to write** most of your articles for you -- for free

6. How to **put your article writing on auto pilot**

7. 10 ways to **increase the perceived value of your article**

8. How to **avoid writer's block** all together

9. How to write articles with just a few clicks of your mouse

10. How to write articles **regardless of your writing ability**

11. How to **write totally original articles**

12. *11 fast and effortless ways* to write articles

13. How to **cut your article writing time** into virtually just a few minutes

14. How to have your articles **practically write themselves**

15. How to write an article by sending *just one simple e-mail message*

16. How to **get free advertising** writing your own articles

17. **6 ways** to persuade other people to **write articles for you for free** or for no upfront costs

☑ **How to Write Hypnotic Joint Venture Proposals**

Shows you how to use hypnotic principles to pull in lucrative joint ventures that produce a huge number of sales, commissions and signups. (**Value: $37**)

Here's just some of the information that's inside...

- The 7 most popular types of joint venture deals. You probably haven't even thought of some of these. *(See Chapter 1)*

- Find out who your first resource should be, plus 18 others people who will want to sell your products for you. *(See Chapter 2)*

- Know exactly what your joint venture prospect needs and wants most from you -- and get a list of 25 specific needs and wants your joint venture prospects have. *(See Chapter 2)*

- Where to find qualified and targeted joint venture partners -- and how to know exactly what they want from you. *(See Chapter 2)*

- How to evaluate a joint venture candidate to make sure they can help you. *(See Chapter 3)*

- How to **pre-sell your hypnotic proposal** before you even send it. *(See Chapter 3)*

- How to **subconsciously** persuade people to accept your proposal -- and the 6 words that will make your offer irresistible. *(See Chapter 4)*

- Know what to say when you are negotiating a joint venture proposal -- even when they want more than you're willing to offer. *(See Chapter 5)*

- How to put the odds in your favor even if they don't accept your offer. *(See Chapter 5)*

- How to get **free products and services** from your joint venture deals. *(See Chapter 6)*

- Get **36 templates** that will influence your prospects to read the rest of your proposal and accept your joint venture offer. These can be altered for any offer. *(See Chapter 6)*

☑ **How to Write Hypnotic Endorsements**

Shows you how to easily write hypnotic endorsements to pull in huge sales, commissions and signups. **(Value: $37)**

Here's just some of the information that's inside...

- How to **pick the most profitable products, services and affiliate programs to endorse**

- **A simple 7 step formula** for writing your very first personal endorsement

- **290 fill in the blank personal endorsement templates** that will allow you to write an endorsement in just minutes

- **20 specific tips** for writing a hypnotic personal endorsement

- How to **transform your personal endorsements into multiple marketing tools**

- 12 ways to **make your endorsements credible** even if you're not an expert

- How to **virtually eliminate your competition** even if you're reselling the same product

☑ **Hypnotic Selling Stories**

Shows you how to easily write hypnotic stories that people relate with, builds their trust in you and increases sales and signups. **(Value: $47)**

Here's a few things you'll learn when you read HSS...

- How to write Hypnotic Selling Stories with little or no writing

- A Step-By-Step Example of How to Create a Hypnotic Selling Story

- What Everyone Will Always Read

- Joe's Secrets for Writing Hypnotic Selling Stories?

- 80 Hypnotic Selling Story Ideas that Sell!

- 58 Formulas for Creating a Hypnotic Selling Story
- How to Turn Your Selling Stories Into Multiple Marketing Tools much, much more...

☑ **Hypnotic Traffic Tools**

Shows you how to use hypnotic tools to generate massive traffic to your websites. **(Value: $47)**

Here's a sneak-peek at a few things you'll find out about...

- The **Amazing Benefits** of Creating Hypnotic Traffic Tools
- The Most Popular Types of *Hypnotic Traffic Tools*
- **15 Places** to Find YOUR Next Hypnotic Traffic Idea
- 12 Reasons People Won't Use Your Hypnotic Traffic Tools
- **99 Ways to Persuade People** to Use Your Hypnotic Traffic Tools
- How to Easily Create Hypnotic Traffic Tools *Without Writing Them Yourself!*
- **16 Important Elements** to Include In Your "Content Requests"
- 10 Places to Send Your "Content Requests"
- *11 Ways to Persuade People to Give Up Their Ideas*

TOTAL VALUE = $620.00

CLICK TO

http://www.HypnoticLibrary.com/g.o/10386

AND ORDER TODAY!

In all, this very special offer brings you a total of **$851.00 worth of products and discounts** -- worth thousands more in true value to you and your business -- for only $397 (plus s/h). And, since we offer a **100%**

unconditional 60-day money-back guarantee, there is no way you can lose with the **Hypnotic Marketing Library Super Package.**

If you want to **take your business to the next level,** you need to increase the effectiveness of every dollar that you spend. With the Hypnotic Marketing Library, you will have all the tools needed to experience:

- Staggering increases in sales and sign-ups

- Out of this world conversion rates

- Sites swamped with free, targeted traffic

- Prospects compelled to reach for their wallet

- Sales letters written quickly and effortlessly

So **get a copy of order Joe Vitale's Hypnotic Marketing Library Super Package** today and save 40% on the most important collection of marketing materials we've ever put together. This one CD-ROM could help you turn your business into a cash machine that *consistently pulls in business,* day after day, month after month. **Order Your Copy Right Now!**

P.S. This offer has a **100% unconditional money-back guarantee.** If you don't see the value in Joe Vitale's *Hypnotic Marketing Library Super Package* on CD-ROM, for any reason whatsoever, you can return it in the first 60 days for a **prompt and courteous refund. So get your package today!**

Here's what the legendary Joe Sugarman says:

"All the tools and phrases are here for even the inexperienced to construct a powerful message. If you're serious about direct marketing, this is a great book to read and study."

JOE VITALE

About the Authors

Dr. Joe Vitale, President of Hypnotic Marketing, Inc., an Internet marketing firm in Texas, has written far too many books to list here. He is the author of the international best-seller, *The Greatest Money-Making Secret in History!*, the best-selling e-book *Hypnotic Writing*, and the best-selling Nightingale-Conant audio program, *The Power of Outrageous Marketing*, and numerous other works.

He is a world-famous copywriter and creator of the "hypnotic writing" method. He has over 15,000 clients internationally. He's appeared on radio, television, infomercials, and in major newspapers across the globe.

He has written books for the American Marketing Association and the American Management Association, including *The AMA Complete Guide to Small Business Advertising* and *There's A Customer Born Every Minute*. His most recent book, co-authored with Jo Han Mok, is *The E-Code: 47 Secrets for Making Money Online Almost Instantly*.

Joe has also created software, such as Hypnotic Writing Wizard and Intention Creator. He recently created a home-study course titled, *Spiritual Marketing: How to Earn $1,000,000 or More This Year Alone*.

Dr. Vitale currently lives in the Hill Country outside of Austin, Texas with his pets and his love, Nerissa.

To browse an online catalog of his books and tapes, to read dozens of free articles by him, or to sign up for his popular free e-newsletter, see his main website at **www.MrFire.com**

"Bene agendo nunquam defessus."

(Never weary of doing good.)

Genevieve Behrend was the only personal pupil of Judge Troward, and she had written the new and practical presentation of the Troward Mental Science, giving the very methods for realizing one's ideals and desires which he himself taught her.

The sages of the ages have united in declaring this great truth: That there is in every human being a source of wisdom and power which we contact through THOUGHT. A Greater Self who can guide and direct us aright. Who can help solve our most vexing problems.

Those who learn to let this Great Self find expression through their lives, find peace, joy, health, success in the truest sense.

Order More Copies of *How to Attain Your Desires* and help change the life of someone else!

Choose from 2 simple ways of ordering today:

1. Visit:

www.morganjamespublishing.com/authors/joe-vitale

or

2. Fill out this order form and return to:

Attain Your Desires
c/o Morgan James Publishing, LLC
Post Office Box 6504
Newport News, Virginia 23606

Name: _____

Address: _____

City: _____ State: _____

Zip: _____ Country: _____

Phone: _____ Quantity: _____

Email: _____

Make Check or US Money Order payable to:
Morgan James Publishing, LLC

$9.95US each (+$3.85US Shipping each)

Printed in the United States
32164LVS00001B/301-324